THE TREE
THE COMPLETE BOOK OF SAXON WITCHCRAFT

This is the complete text of the Saxon Witches *Book of Shadows* which was written down for the first time during the Persecutions so that their rituals would not be lost. Raymond Buckland, a recognized authority in the field and leader of the religion for over a decade, introduces the text with historical background, descriptions of the Saxon deities, and explanations of their primary beliefs. Apart from annotating the text, Mr. Buckland also supplies information on the Magical Runic Alphabet of the Saxons, a selection of original Pagan songs, and Seax-Wican recipes for intoxicants.

The Tree: The Complete Book of Saxon Witchcraft gives instructions for initiation ceremonies, the eight Sabbats, marriage, birth and death rites. The art and practice of Saxon Galdra or Magic is explained as well as Hwata (Divination) and Lacnunga (Herbal Lore) so that they can be used for protection, love potions, and healing.

The Seax-Wica do not have an Oath of Secrecy per se. Their "Rite of Self-Dedication" allows interested individuals to form their own covens and initiate themselves into the Craft. *The Tree: The Complete Book of Saxon Witchcraft* presents the necessary information so that this process can be performed in a true and proper Pagan manner.

By the same author
ANATOMY OF THE OCCULT

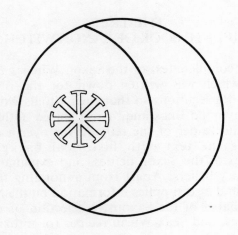

Symbol of the Seax-Wica

Symbolizing the Sun, the Moon, and the eight Sabbats, or "The Wheel of the Year."

THE TREE

THE COMPLETE BOOK
OF
SAXON WITCHCRAFT

BY RAYMOND BUCKLAND

The *Seax-Wica* "Book of Shadows", with annotations
and additional material by Raymond Buckland.

SAMUEL WEISER
York Beach, Maine

For Taza

First published in 1974 by
Samuel Weiser, Inc.
P.O. Box 612
York Beach, ME 03910

Fifth printing, 1985

ISBN 0-87728-258-7
Library of Congress Catalog Card No. 74-79397

Printed in the U.S.A. by
Mitchell-Shear, Inc.
Ann Arbor, MI

CONTENTS

Introduction   1

Historical Background   5

Beliefs
    Deities   11
    Woden   14
    Freya   18
    Reincarnation   22
    Retribution   25

Hierarchy   26

Circle, Tools and Dress   30

Officers   34

The Book   36

The Rites   37
    Erecting the Temple   38
    Clearing the Temple   41
    Self-Dedication   42
    Initiation   45
    Esbat   50
    Full Moon   52
    Cakes and Ale   54

Sabbats   57
Samhain Sabbat   59
Yule Sabbat   62
Imbolc Sabbat   64
Spring Sabbat   66
Beltane Sabbat   69
Midsummer Sabbat   72
Lughnasadh Sabbat   74
Autumn Sabbat   76
Hand-Fasting   78
Hand-Parting   82
Birth Rite   85
Crossing the Bridge (at Death)   88
Consecration   91

Additional Material

Galdra (Magick)   93
    Protection From Evil   94
    Love   96
    Healing   101
    Other Magick   104

Hwata (Divination)   106
    The Saxon Wands   107
    Tarot   109
    The Path   110
    Scrying   112
    Crystal-Gazing   113
    Mirror-Gazing   115
    Fire-Fantasy   116

Lacnunga (Herbal Lore)   117
    The Gathering, Drying and Keeping of Simples and
        their juices   118
    The Way of Making and Keeping all Necessary
        Compounds   122

Appendix 'A' — Magickal Alphabets   129

Appendix 'B' – Seax-Wican Songs   138

Appendix 'C' –
   Seax-Wica Recipes for Wine, Beer, and Ale   149

Appendix 'D' – Paganism   153

Bibliography   156

Introduction

Today there is a tremendous interest in the Occult in general, and in Witchcraft in particular. There are several reasons for this, the main one being the form of education received by young people today. They are taught to be inquisitive. Gone are the days when they would accept as "gospel" whatever was handed to them by teacher or by parent. Now they will take what is handed to them and examine it. They will look at it from all angles; they will question. They will perhaps finally accept, but they are just as likely to reject. This is true of all things, including religion. And this is as it should be.

Under this close scrutiny many of the long-established religions have been found wanting. There is a general dissatisfaction with organized religion in its present form. There is, therefore, a searching for alternatives.

These two factors—the investigatory approach and the rejection of long-standing religious forms—have coincided with the time of Witchcraft's re-emergence. Only within the last twenty-five years has Witchcraft been able to come out into the open again and declare itself for what it really is—another religion, albeit the "Old Religion", one of Man's first. So those who were searching have suddenly discovered that there is, in fact, an alternative. And to most of them it looks an extremely attractive alternative.

Witchcraft is not an "anti-religion". It is not anti-Christian (not Satanism); it is not anti anything. It is simply a nature-based religion in its own right, dating from pre-Christian times. To the early Christian, however, anything that was *non*-Christian was automatically *anti*-Christian and to be done away with. So for centuries we have been foisted with stories of ugly old Witches working evil magick in the service of the Devil (as it happens Witches don't even believe in the Devil). But with the repeal in 1951 of the last law against Witchcraft in England the way was finally opened for the Witches to present their side of the story. The first actual Witch to do this was the late Dr. Gerald B. Gardner, with his book *Witchcraft Today* (London, 1954)—still the finest work on the subject.

Finding, then, that there was another religious possibility, those who were searching started to investigate. But investigation was not easy, for the *Wicca* (Witchcraft) is a Mystery Religion. The word "Mystery" comes from the Greek *meuin*, meaning "to keep mum; to keep silent". A feature of Mystery Religions is, therefore, an Oath of Secrecy. Of the many Mystery Religions of ancient Greece and Rome today we know little in the way of details, due to this oath taken by the adherents. So with Witchcraft. Those trying to investigate it are hampered in that much of the Wiccan liturgy is just not available to non-Initiates.[1] Such writers as Gerald Gardner did present enough information, however, to give a good indication of the

---

[1] One woman recently published what she claimed were the complete rituals of a British tradition of Witchcraft. She felt she could publish them since she was "not bound by the British Oath of Secrecy". She was obviously ignorant of the fact that the Oath is not one of any particular nationality but of the religion itself.

type of rituals, rites, beliefs, etc., followed in "the Craft".

As a Nature-based religion it is attractive today to the ecology minded. As a religion simple and uncomplicated in its rites it appeals to those who dislike the higher esoteric symbolism, the pomp and ceremony, of some Churches' rites. As a religion of participation (due to restriction of numbers within each group, or "coven") it appeals to a great many seeking such personal involvement. As a religion of equality of the sexes it appeals to many women who feel there should be more such equality. Yet despite this general appeal, despite this discovery of what seems the ideal, perhaps previously undreamed-of, religion it turns out to be unavailable to many. Why? Mainly because it is not a proselytizing religion.

Witches do not set out to convert others to their ways. They feel there can be no *one* religious way suitable for *every*one. One person should not try to force his religion on another. Witches feel that those who are "right" for the Craft will eventually find it, even if it does turn out to be a long, somewhat frustrating, search. So covens do not advertise themselves.

Even when contact is made with a coven there is not immediate entry for the would-be Witch. Because of the many misconceptions that still abound time must be taken to verify that the newcomer is *bona-fide* in wanting to join as a worshipper of the Old Gods. Those seeking devil-worship, drugs, and/or orgies are turned away. This absence of immediate entry has created an interesting phenomena—the mushrooming of numerous spurious "Witches" and "Covens", along with the appearance of a number of books on "How to be a Witch" and "How to form a Coven".

As in Christianity there are many denominations (e.g. Baptist, Methodist, Episcopal, Roman Catholic, etc.), so in Witchcraft are there many traditions (e.g. Celtic,

Druidic, Welsh, Irish, Gardnerian, Norse, etc.). Where most of the Wiccan traditions are concerned it is no more possible to start a coven from scratch and elect yourself to the Priesthood (without the necessary lengthy training) than it would be to start your own Catholic Church and elect yourself Priest, Monsignor, Bishop, or whatever. Perhaps the single, solitary, exception to this statement is the Saxon Tradition of Witchcraft—the *Seax-Wica*.

Although still a branch of the Mystery Religion of the Wicca the *Seax-Wica* do not have an Oath of Secrecy *per se*. They have a "Rite of Self-Dedication", which serves a similar, though not identical, purpose. This means that their rites *are* available for study. It means that those searching for the Craft *can* have ready access to at least one branch, or tradition, of it.

So to fill this great need by so many seeking to belong to the Craft, I here present in full, for the first time in print, the Saxon Witches' "Book of Shadows",[2] known to them as *The Tree*. With this, and the explanatory material, it is now possible to do what I just said, above, cannot generally be done: to Initiate yourself as a Witch, and to start your own Coven.

Raymond Buckland

---

[2] Until the time of the Persecutions the Craft was a purely oral tradition. During the Persecutions covens made a point of losing contact with one another so that should one coven be caught, even under torture they could not give away another coven. With this separation of the groups it was decided to put the rituals themselves into writing, so that they would not be lost. This was done in a book known as The Book of Shadows—since it was a time of meeting "in the shadows". Unfortunately, the books are generally sadly incomplete so far as theological thoughts are concerned.

Historical Background

During the fourth and fifth centuries a movement took place in Western Europe known as the "Wandering of the Nations". Tribes of Goths, Vandals, Suevi, Alans, and others passed out from their old homes in the north and northeast and moved into the territory of the Roman Empire. For the previous two centuries Germans had been crossing back and forth between Germany and the Roman Empire, but now for the first time whole tribes began to migrate at once. The Visigoths (West Goths) passed into southern Gaul and Spain; Burgundians into southeastern Gaul; Franks into northern Gaul; Vandals into Africa; Ostrogoths (East Goths), and later Lombards (Long Beards), into Italy. One group of peoples, however, did not go southward but westward. And they travelled not by land but by water. These were the Angles, Saxons, and Jutes, who sailed out into the North Sea and sought the islands of Britain.

These tribes differed in many important particulars from the others of the "Wandering Nations". They had lived in a portion of Germany most remote from the influence of Roman customs and ideas. They lived in lands that were densely wooded, damp, and cold. Rivers were almost the only highways. Clearings in the forests were the only dwelling-places. The Jutes lived in modern Jutland north of the river Schley, the Angles in the region south of the Jutes and along the shore of the North Sea. The Saxons were a Teutonic race whose name is generally thought to be derived from the Old German word *sahs* (a knife, or short sword). They are first mentioned by Ptolemy in the second century A.D. He speaks of them as inhabiting a district bounded by the Eide, the Elbe, and the Trave—in northern Germany, from the base of the Danish Peninsula to the mouth of the Rhine.

In the third century of the Christian era the Saxons were a numerous, warlike, yet practical people. In the fifth century considerable hordes of them crossed from the Continent and laid the foundations of the Saxon kingdoms in Britain—Essex, or East Saxons; Middlesex, or Middle Saxons; Sussex, or South Saxons; and Wessex, or West Saxons. The West Saxons called themselves *Gewissi*, and included many lesser groups such as the Dorsaetas, Wiltsaetas, Sumorsaetas, Defonas, Wentsaetas, Magonsaetas, and Hwiccas (*saete* = sitter; dweller).

For a hundred years before their migration to the British Isles the Saxons and their neighbors had been seafarers and plunderers on the coasts of the North Sea. As early as 364 A.D. they had been heard of in Britain, and the Romans there had established a special official—the Count of the Saxon Shore—to guard the coast, from the Wash to Pevensey, against their attack.

The invasion of Britain by the Saxons (plus the Angles and Jutes) marked the beginning of the British national history by destroying the Roman civilization in Britain and establishing the English race and nation with its own distinctive language, society, institutions, and government. They were Pagans, inferior to the Romans, yet they were most assuredly not barbarians. They understood the Roman civilization but discarded it as unsuited to essentially agricultural communities. T.C. Lethbridge, in *Merlin's Island*, points out that "although we call these people Anglo-Saxons, we can be by no means certain that they did not almost instantly become a hybrid race. . . . In most cases I believe that the immigrants married a high percentage of British women and that, in a generation or two the whole material culture had altered as a result of it."

The Saxons had travelled across to England in light, open, boats made of osiers covered with skins sewed together. They were weighed down with their worldly possessions: ploughs, harrows, farming implements, along with bronze-bound wooden buckets, pots, bowls, and even livestock. Initially they gathered together in small hamlets made up of clusters of huts. The huts themselves were usually circular in plan and sunk two or three feet into the ground.[1]

Although the Saxons had fine elaborate textiles for their "best" clothing their more usual, everyday, wear was plain and simple. The men sometimes wore cross-gartered, loose trousers, but were just as likely to be bare-legged and bare-footed. They wore simple tunic tops of coarse homespun cloth. The women wore equally simple tunics held at the waist by a girdle, and at the shoulders by brooches. From the girdle might hang characteristic T-shaped bronze trinkets, ivory rings, etc.. They would probably have a knife (*seax*) stuck in the girdle. The men, too, would have a knife stuck in their wide leather belts. Their weapons were homemade and included a rough, six-foot spear—carried by most men—and occasionally a flat, double-edged, sword. This latter had a blade approximately thirty inches in length and two-and-a-half inches wide. Two feet in diameter circular, wooden, shields, with ridged iron bosses in the middle, might also be carried.

During the first two centuries of the settlement the conquerers of Britain were not single powerful tribes

[1] See *Witchcraft From the Inside*, Buckland, Llewellyn, 1971, page 93.

establishing single tribal kingdoms, but rather dozens of small tribal groups each under its own war leader. Some of them were groups of warriors, but many were doubtless groups of kin-families; that is, families connected by ties of blood, composed of women, children, and slaves. In nearly all the early groups the war-leader, or *heretoga*, became the king. He was awarded the largest portion of the conquered lands and the largest share of the booty. His family was, supposedly, descended from the gods.

By degrees the Saxons took possession of almost the whole country south of Hadrian's Wall. Eventually there arose seven main kingdoms, which are commonly called the *Saxon Heptarchy*: Kent, Sussex, Wessex, Essex, East Anglia, Mercia, and Northumberland.

The English were characterized by their intense love of freedom, their reliance upon the ties of kinship, and their inherent capacity for cooperation and unity. In Britain they instituted a complete system of self government which became, in practice, a rude constitutional monarchy conducted by a King and a *Witan* (or national council). This Witan was composed chiefly of *eorls*, or nobles of hereditary rank; and *gesiths*, or professional warriors (who afterwards formed a lower nobility as *thegns*, or *thanes*, by acquiring minimum holdings of land). The main body of the people ranked as *ceorls*, or free land-owners, but there was also a large class of serfs, or *theows*, composed of prisoners of war and men enslaved through debt or crime.

Methods of life and government had, by the close of Eadgar's reign, become well established. A king of one of the tribes had eventually become king of all England. The king's powers were far from absolute. He was first and foremost a warrior, the head of the people in arms, for conquest had been, up to this time, one of the most important aspects of Anglo-Saxon life. As a law-maker, whether in writing down the old laws or in making new ones, he generally acted with his chief advisors—the Witan. There are many instances to show that the Witan could elect the king, but few to show that they could depose him. Alfred and his Witan made peace with Guthrum; but no mention is made of the Witan when, a few years later, Eadward made a similar peace. A little later, however, Aethelred and the Witan entered into a peace with Olaf and the Danish army. In general it seems that the Witan did not act without the cooperation of the king, nor the king without the advice and consent of the Witan.

EARLY ANGLO-SAXON KINGS

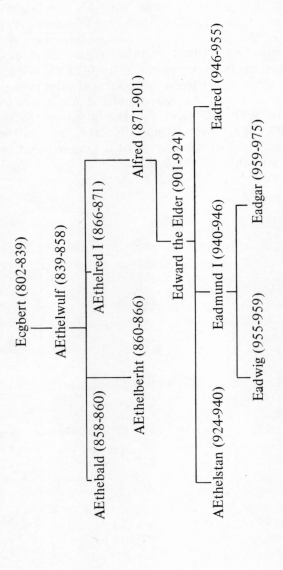

Ecgbert (802-839)

AEthelwulf (839-858)

AEthebald (858-860)

AEthelberht (860-866)

AEthelred I (866-871)

Alfred (871-901)

Edward the Elder (901-924)

AEthelstan (924-940)

Eadmund I (940-946)

Eadred (946-955)

Eadwig (955-959)

Eadgar (959-975)

Beliefs

Deities

The Saxons were practicing pagans during at least their first five generations in England. They worshipped four principal deities: Woden, Thunor, Tiw, and Frig or Freya. Since their temples, like their houses, were built of wood they have not survived, though their locations and those of their open-air meeting-places—groves, etc.—have. Throughout Britain today may be found innumerable place-names indicative of the deities worshipped and/or the locations of former shrines to these deities.

Brian Branston, in *The Lost Gods of England* (Thames and Hudson, London, 1957) says, ". . . usually, no opponents fight more bitterly and to the death than warring religions. True, the winner will sometimes wear its opponent's creeds like scalps—but not around the waist: every effort is made to obliterate the memory of whence the creed came and the scalp is worn like a toupé and passed off as real hair. The Christian religion had done this in the very beginning when it was struggling for dear life against the Hellenistic faiths of the eastern Mediterranean and Christ was duelling with Attis and Adonis and Osiris and especially Mithras; Christianity adopted alien ideas again when in England

11

the missionary monks acted on the advice of Pope Gregory and incorporated local heathen customs into the conduct of the Christian year. Once Christianity was accepted in England the Church had no compunction about obliterating the memory of the heathen origin while retaining the custom of Yule-tide and harvest festivals for instance, or of the charming (now *blessing*) of the plough. The obliteration of heathenism from written records (not so from the lips of men) was particularly easy. It was easy because reading and writing were a Church monopoly with the result that what heathen literary memories remain have done so largely due to oversight. It is not to be expected that the writers in the cool cell and shady cloister would lend their quills to propaganda of the heathen gods. And because we moderns subscribe to the belief (or pretend we do) that 'the pen is mightier than the sword', we are apt to discount evidence which is unwritten, except where such evidence is of itself conclusive and verifiable from written sources: one of our modern shibboleths is that we must have everything in writing. It is a good thing that our pagan ancestors have, so to speak, writ large their heathendom on the English landscape. The gods of the English still in place-names retain a firm hold on the countryside."

Chief amongst the gods of the Saxons was Woden, and there are far more mentions of him in English place-names than of any of the other deities: Wansdyke (*Wodnes dic*), an earthwork, runs all the way from Hampshire to Somerset; *Wodnes beorh* (Woden's barrow) is close by, as is *Wodnes denu* (Woden's valley). In other areas are found "Woden's plain", "Woden's fortress", Woodnesborough, and Wornshill.

Freya was chief amongst the female deities. She too is found in Freefolk, Froyle, Fryup, Frydaythorpe, and Frobury.

Branston, again, mentions "Three Old English words attest the strength of heathen worship in the land by the widespread frequency with which they occur: they are *ealh* a temple, *hearh* or *hearg* a hill sanctuary, and *weoh* which means shrine or sacred spot. *Ealh* is rarer than the others but may still be found in Alkham near Dover; it occurred too in Ealhfleot an early name of a channel connecting Faversham with the sea. *Hearh* remains in Harrow-on-the-Hill (Middlesex), Harrowden (Bedford, Northants, Essex), Arrowfield Top (Worcestershire) and Peper Harrow (Surrey). Most common of all and most widely distributed is *weoh* which lives on in Wye (Kent), Whiligh, Whyly, Willey (Surrey), Wheely Down, Weyhill (Hants), Weedon Beck, Weedon Lois (Northants.), Weedon (Bucks.), Weoley (Worcs.), Weeley (Essex), Wyville (Kesteven), Weeford (Staffs.), Wyham (Lincs.), and Patchway (Sussex)."

WODEN and FREYA were the two most important and most widely worshipped deities. These are the deities whose names are honored in the rites of Saxon Witchcraft today. Woden, of course, is especially remembered in the weekday "Wednesday"—Woden's Day (*Wodnes-daeg*); and Freya in "Friday"—Freya's Day (the other days were: Sunday for the Sun; Monday for the Moon; Tuesday for Tuisco, or Tiw; Thursday for Thor; Saturday for Saterne).

Woden

The primitive west Europeans had called the god Wodenaz. This later developed into Wuotan (Old High German) and Wodan (Old Saxon). It is generally believed that he was first thought of as a sky deity—perhaps a wind or storm god—with great wisdom, and with some sort of powers over life and death. This may be evidenced by the derivation of Wodenaz from an Indo-European word, parent also of the Sanskrit *vata* and the Latin *ventus*, both meaning "wind". He could be compared to the Hindu Lord of the Wind, Vata, and the German storm giant Wode.

Woden had great skill as a magician or sorcerer (*Galdorcraeftig* = "a person proficient in magick"), and also as a shape-shifter. His skill is seen in one of the oldest existing pieces of Anglo-Saxon verse containing the *Nine Herbs Charm*:

"The snake came crawling and struck at none. But Woden took nine glory-twigs[1] and struck the adder so that it flew into nine parts . . ."

[1] Pieces of wood on which were carved runic inscriptions.

Woden appears in Norse mythology as Odin, the supreme deity, son of Borr and Bestla. He presided over the assemblage of the gods and over their feasts, consuming nothing but wine. As the wisest of the gods he obtained his wisdom from two ravens named *Hugin* ("thought") and *Munin* ("memory"), who perched on his shoulders. The ravens could fly through all the reaches of the universe and would tell Odin (Woden) what they had seen. Two wolves were also his constant companions.

Woden was bearded, wore a long cloak and either a hood or a floppy-brimmed hat. He leaned upon a huge spear as he walked. He it was who introduced the runic form of writing. In the Old Norse verse *Lay of the High One* (stanzas 138, 139 and 141) he says:

"I trow that I hung
on the windy tree,
   swung there nights all of nine;
gashed with a blade
bloodied by Odin (Woden),
   myself an offering to myself
knotted to that tree
no man knows
   whither the root of it runs.

None gave me bread
None gave me drink,
   down to the depths I peered
to snatch up runes
with a roaring screech
   and fall in a dizzied faint!

Wellbeing I won
and wisdom too,
   and grew and joyed in my growth;
from a word to a word
I was led to a word
   from a deed to another deed."

The Woden of the Saxons was not quite the same personage as the Odin of the Viking Age (also, incidentally, the Old English *waelcyrge* were vastly different from the Norse Valkyrie). Woden was not concerned with organizing battalions of slain warriors, but more with walking the rolling downs and watching over his (living) people.

By the sixth century magicians and sorcerers had a good working knowledge of writing, useful in their secret arts. The writing generally used was the Runic[2] discovered by Woden. One of the earliest examples of these runes is found on the Saxon cross now preserved in the apse of Ruthwell church, Dumfriesshire.

It is sometimes referred to as the "Futhorc", after the first six letters that appear there. It is also referred to thus, today, to distinguish it from some of the later variations of the runes. These main ones were Anglo-Saxon, Scandinavian, and Germanic. The Celtic peoples of England adopted, and adapted, the Saxon variety and a form of runic writing is used in many traditions of Witchcraft today. The *Seax-Wica*, however, stick to the original "futhorc" (see Appendix A).

---

[2] In the Anglo-Saxon epic poem, *Beowulf*, there is mention of an ancient sword hilt which had a story cut into it in runes. This story was a pre-Christian version of the flood.

ᚠ f ᚢ u ᚦ th ᚩ o ᚱ r ᚳ c

ᚷ g ᚹ w ᚻ h ᚾ n ᛁ i

ᚸ gh ᛋ s ᛏ t

ᛒ b ᛖ e ᛗ m ᛚ l ᛝ ng ᛟ oe

ᛞ d ᚪ a ᚫ ae

ᚣ y ᛠ ea ᛣ k v

Freya

Freya was born of Nerthus (Mother Earth), but later took on herself many of the attributes of her mother. The name Freya means "Lady". She is regarded as the equivalent of the Greek Aphrodite and the Roman Venus; a goddess of Love, a mother, a protectress of children and of women in childbirth. She is referred to in Norse mythology as "most lovely of the goddesses".

Snorri Sturluson, in the *Prose Edda* (1241), gives many details of the gods and includes a myth of Freya in search of her sacred necklace "Brisingamen" (This necklace, or torque, was named after the Brisings, the dwarves who made it. It is mentioned in *Beowulf*). Briefly Loki, the Mischief-Maker of the gods, stole Brisingamen (*Brosingamene*) from Freya and placed it on a rock, where it was later discovered by the god Heimdall. He retrieved it, after a fight with Loki, and carried it back to Asgard to restore to Freya.

Obviously, in this myth, Brisingamen represents fertility, or the spirit of vegetation. Its loss leads to the Fall and Winter months; its retrieval to the Spring and Summer. Similar myths are found elsewhere: Sif's loss of her golden tresses; Idunn's loss of her golden apples; variations on the theme of Ishtar's descent into the

18

Underworld in her search for Tammuz. The actual Myth of the Goddess of Saxon Witchcraft[3] is as follows:

"1: All day had Freya, most lovely of the goddesses, played and romped in the fields. Then did she lay down to rest.

2: And while she slept deft Loki, the Prankster, the Mischief-Maker of the Gods, did espy the glimmering of *Brosingamene*, formed of Gladra[4], her constant companion. Silent as night did Loki move to the Goddess' side and, with fingers formed[5] over the very ages in lightness[6], did remove the silver circlet[7] from about her snow-white neck.

3: Straightway did Freya arouse, on sensing its loss. Though he moved with the speed of the winds yet Loki she glimpsed as he passed swiftly from sight into the Barrow that leads to Drëun[8].

4: Then was Freya in despair. Darkness descended all about her to hide her tears. Great was her anguish. All light, all life, all creatures joined in her doom.

5: To all corners were sent the Searchers, in quest of Loki; yet knew they, they would find him not. For who is there may descend into Drëun

---

[3] *cf.* The Myth of the Goddess of Gardnerian/Celtic Witchcraft as given in *Witchcraft Today* (Gardner, London, 1954).

[4] Magick

[5] trained

[6] lightness of touch; dexterity

[7] This would seem to indicate a solid torque, rather than a chain or similar.

[8] Land of the Dead, beneath the Earth.

and return again from thence?

6: Excepting the gods themselves and, alack, mischievous Loki.

7: So it was that, still weak from grief, Freya herself elected to descend in search of *Brosingamene*. At the portals of the Barrow was she challenged yet recognized and passed.

8: The multitude of souls within cried joyfully to see her, yet could she not tarry as she sought her stolen light[9].

9: The infamous Loki left no trail to follow, yet was he everywhere past seen[10]. Those to whom she spake held to Freya (that) Loki carried no jewel as he went by.

10: Where, then, was it hid?

11: In despair she searched an age.

12: Hearhden[11], the mighty Smith of the Gods[12], did arise from his rest to sense the bewailment of the souls to Freya's sorrow. Striding from his smithy, to find the cause of the sorrow, did he espy the Silver Circlet where Loki Mischief-Maker had laid it: upon the rock before his door.

13: Then was all clear.

14: As Hearhden took hold of *Brosingamene* (then did) Loki appear before him, his face wild with rage.

15: Yet would Loki not attack Hearhden, this Mighty Smith whose strength was known even beyond Drëun.

16: By whiles and tricks did he strive to get his

---

[9] Probably referring to the shining brilliance of the necklace.

[10] Had just been seen.

[11] Heimdall

[12] cf. Haephaestos of Greek mythology.

hands upon the (silver) circlet. He shape-shifted[13]; he darted here and there; he was visible, then invisible. Yet could he not sway the Smith.

17: Tiring of the fight[14] Hearhden raised his mighty club[15]. Then sped Loki away.

18: Great was the joy of Freya when Hearhden placed *Brosingamene* once more about her snow-white neck.

19: Great were the cries of joy from Dreun and above.

20: Great were the thanks that Freya, and all Men, gave to the gods for the return of *Brosing-amene*."

*   *   *

The worship of a God and a Goddess ties in Saxon Witchcraft with other traditions of the Craft as being essentially a Nature religion. Everywhere in Nature is found a system of male and female; because that is the way of the Gods—a God and a Goddess—believe the Witches. No all-male or all-female deity. It is, then, a duotheistic religion. It stems, as has been well pointed out in such works as Murray's *God of the Witches*, Lethbridge's *Witches*, and this author's *Witchcraft From the Inside*, from early man's animistic beliefs. With man's original belief in many deities the two most important to his existence were a (horned) God of Hunting—later to become a (foliate) God of Nature generally—and a Goddess of Fertility. To the *Seax-Wica* these are now Woden and Freya.

---

[13] Changed shape, to appear as something or someone else.

[14] the "antics of Loki", since this was not a real fight.

[15] The club of Herakles?

21

Reincarnation

Along with other traditions the *Seax-Wica* believe in
reincarnation. It is a progressive reincarnation. Always
in human form, each life will be better in some way
than the previous one. There is no separate Heaven and
Hell in the Craft philosophy. At death your Spirit goes
to one place, known as The Summerland. This is
traditionally thought to be, vaguely, "to the East". The
Seax-Wica sometimes refer to it as *Drĕun*. Originally
Drĕun was thought to be beneath the earth, its entrance
being through a barrow. Today, however, there are few
of the Saxon tradition who still think of it as being
necessarily underground.

In Drĕun you rest and relax. There are reunions with
past friends and loved ones, of course, and there are
meetings with the God and Goddess to plan your future
life or lives. Eventually, when the time is right, you are
reborn through the agencies of the Goddess into a new
body on this earth. A number of such lives are gone
through. In each one something necessary to your
development is learned or experienced. The lives may be
long or short, depending on how quickly the necessary
learning or experience is dealt with. Usually there is no
memory of a previous life during the present one.

Occasionally, however, there is and occasionally there is a "carrying forward" of previously amassed knowledge. This latter, the *Seax-Wica* feel, explains such phenomena as child prodigies. They feel there are usually seven incarnations undergone. It could be less, though this seems seldom to be so, in the case of a Spirit or Soul who learns quickly. Or it could be more, in the case of a slow learner.

There are new Spirits, or Souls, starting all the time, so any cross-section would show a certain number of "new Souls" along with the various "old Souls". It is felt that the theory of reincarnation explains many cases of *déjà-vu*—the feeling that you have been somewhere before. Not all instances can be explained this way, of course, but certainly a very large percentage.

In company with all Witches the *Seax-Wica* have little concern for the body after death. It is the Spirit, or Soul, which continues. The body was just a shell for a particular lifetime. Some Witches favor cremation at death, and are almost violently opposed to the high-cost funerals foisted on unsuspecting mourners by the funeral trade[16]. More and more Witches are willing their bodies at death to hospitals, for research purposes. The ideal, some Saxons feel, would be the burial of the lifeless body in a simple basketwork coffin, or the like. In this way it could be easily absorbed back into the earth as it decomposed. Quite a reversal of the "life everlasting" lead-lined (highly expensive) coffins designed to contain the body in lifelike form as long as possible.

What happens at the end of the seven-life cycle? No one really knows for sure. When the *Book of Shadows* first came into being there was much that was still not written in it, but was passed on orally. Many of these

---

[16] *cf The American Way of Death*, Jessica Mitford.

oral traditions eventually became lost over the passing centuries. Another good example of this loss, is the Craft thoughts on the creation of the world.

Retribution

Many, if not most, Witch traditions believe in retribution in the present life. There is no thought of "putting things off" till some big Judgement Day when you will receive your just rewards or punishments. No. In Witch beliefs you get back, at three times the magnitude, whatever you do ... be it Good or be it Evil. This (hopefully) causes you to stop and think about what you do, and the possible effects of your actions on others.

The *Seax-Wica* follow this general belief. They do feel, though, that you are entitled to help things along a little when it comes to protecting yourself. For example, should someone (obviously a non-Witch) be working against you in some magickal or non-magickal way, rather than just sitting back and waiting for them to get their own back—which might mean that you suffer in the meantime as a result of their actions—you can certainly set up protection for yourself. Something which will not only protect you but will also help send back the other's evil. They feel that in doing so they are acting as instruments of the gods. They would never, however, be the initial protagonists.

Hierarchy

Most Craft traditions have a High Priest and/or a High Priestess. In many traditions the High Priestess is the more important of the two. In fact in the Gardnerian tradition although it is possible for a meeting to be held without the High Priest being present it is impossible to hold one without the High Priestess. With the Gardnerians the High Priest is really nothing more than a glorified Altar-boy—as this author has pointed out many times in the past.

In the *Seax-Wica* there can be a High Priest *or* a High Priestess—each quite able to function alone should the other not be present—or both acting together, each *equally* important. But let us start at the bottom of the scale, as it were, and work up.

First, there are those who do not actually belong to the (Saxon) Craft. These are called *Theows*, singular: *Theow*—pronounced "th-ō" ("th" as in *thing*). It is permissible for Theows to attend ritual meetings, though only by invitation. In many traditions none but the initiated may attend these meetings and so the only way a would-be Witch can get a "taste" of a Circle is through some such Outer Circle organization as The Pagan Way[1] . But with Saxon Witchcraft a non-Initiate

[1]   see Appendix D

may attend as a guest, should all the coven be in agreement. This guest is then a Theow.

Having been to one or more meetings perhaps the Theow then wishes to become a full member. He or she would then be placed in some sort of training program and become known as a *Ceorl* (pronounced "cawl"), a neophyte. This leads to eventual initiation. It is usually a member of the opposite sex who is appointed as the Ceorl's teacher. This might be the High Priest(ess) but it need not necessarily be so. The training program consists mainly of steering the Ceorl to read what are considered the "better" books on the Craft and its background (see *Bibliography*). The Ceorl is encouraged to question and to seek answers and is also trained in the use of the Witch Tools, the Hierarchy of the Coven, Herbal Lore, and Divination. Of these last two merely an introduction would be given.

Eventually a date would be set for Initiation. This might be as soon as one month after first meeting the Coven as a Theow, or it might be as long as a year. The period would depend entirely upon the readiness (in terms of learning) of the Ceorl, and the space available within the Coven.[2]

The *Seax-Wica*, as with most traditions, prefer to have equal numbers of males and females in their covens. It is not always possible to have such an ideal, however, so there are many covens with more of one sex than the other. The Saxons do not, again as some others do, have "partners". Each is there as an individual. This helps, of course, when one person is given the job of training a Ceorl. It means there is no "partner" left out.

Although it seems unlikely that a homosexual would be attracted to a religion which is definitely male-female based, it does sometimes happen. If this should be the

---

[2] It is unlikely that anyone would be accepted as a Ceorl unless there were a definite vacancy in the Coven.

case then Saxon Witchcraft seems more able to "absorb" than many of the other traditions. (It is not unknown for homosexuals, or lesbians, to work together exclusively as a *Seax-Wican* coven; or to blend quite happily with others.)

Once initiated you are known as a *Gesith* (soft "g" as in "gentle"). There are no "degrees of advancement". Every Saxon Witch is a Gesith. From among the Gesiths the Priest and Priestess are chosen. They will reign as such for at least thirteen moons (one year). At the end of that time the Coven may ask them to continue for another Span. Or it may be that someone else is suggested, or suggests him/herself to take over the position. If this is so the Coven will vote on it, either openly or in secret ballot (they *should* be able to discuss the pros and cons of any member quite openly and without malice). Should a contestant not be voted in, over the "old" Priest(ess), there are certainly no hard feelings. Many Priests and Priestesses rule for many years, some contested each year, some never contested. Should there be a tie in the voting the incumbent automatically continues. When one has ruled for more than one Span, even if not consecutively, one is known as a *High* Priest(ess). In this way it is possible to tell the experienced Priesthood from the new.

This form of accession to the Priesthood, found in the *Seax-Wica*, has one thing in particular to recommend it. It means that no one person can become "all-powerful". In some of the other Craft traditions the High Priest, or High Priestess, can develop bad cases of egoism and egotism. This has led to numerous claims, such as "Queen of All the Witches", "Witch King", etc., and has contributed to much bitterness within what should be an essentially joyful religion.

It is possible for a Gesith to break away and form a new coven *at any time*. This sometimes happens when someone is unsuccessful in challenging the High Priest(ess) at the end of a Span. But it does not happen this way as often as one might think. The more usual reason for a coven's splitting is just that it has got too many members and is seeking to expand. Or it might be due to relocation of one or more of its members.

In virtually all other traditions a coven cannot just be started from scratch—in other words a group of people cannot suddenly decide that they are going to be Witches and form a coven. To become a Witch, in other traditions, you must be initiated by a member of the Priesthood; to become of the Priesthood yourself you must undergo several years training. The *Seax-Wica* is probably the sole exception to this form of entry and advancement.

With the *Seax-Wica* it is preferred that you go the course of Theow, Ceorl, and (through Initiation) Gesith; but it *is* possible to perform a rite of "Self-Dedication"—in other words, a Self Initiation—and start your own coven. This is because the Saxons realize that there are a great many people searching, in vain, for contact with the Craft. They therefore try to make the Craft a little more accessible to such earnest seekers. (It is also a hang-over from the early days of Witchcraft when there were many people living in isolated areas completely cut-off from others. Geographical cut-off from a coven did not then mean that worship was impossible. So, in those days, there were many who performed the rite of Self-Dedication, that they might still worship the gods.)

There are no Degrees of Advancement within the *Seax-Wica*. You are either a Gesith or a Priest(ess). From amongst the Gesiths certain coven officials may be chosen (see below). There are also no main leaders of this branch of the Craft—no King, no Queen, no Grand High Priestess, or whatever. The covens are completely autonomous. There is no Vow of Secrecy, and *The Tree* (Book of Shadows) is accessible to all—hence its publication here. The *Seax-Wica* is therefore not a Mystery Religion in the true sense of the word.

Circle, Tools and Dress

In common with all Craft traditions the *Seax-Wica* meet in a Circle. This is nine feet in diameter. A traditional size used solely to limit the physical size of the working area and, therefore, the maximum number of coven members. This maximum would be about a dozen. This is felt to be a "comfortable" size for compatibility—there should be complete harmony within the coven (in Gardnerian Witchcraft the Circle is also nine feet in diameter, but for a definite magickal reason).

In the center of the Circle is the Altar, which should be circular. When meeting out-of-doors a rock or a tree-stump would be ideal for the purpose. There are certain "tools" kept on the Altar top, and others are held by the Witches themselves. At the center back of the Altar stands a single tall white candle. Figures to represent the God and Goddess (Woden and Freya) may be placed on either side of it. Before the candle stands the censer. On one side of the censer stands a dish of water together with a dish of salt, and on the other side stand drinking-horns, or goblets, for the Priest and Priestess. Across the center of the Altar lies the Sword and before it, facing the Priest(ess), is the green-covered book known as *The Tree*. Spaced around the Circle itself are lighted candles. their number and relative

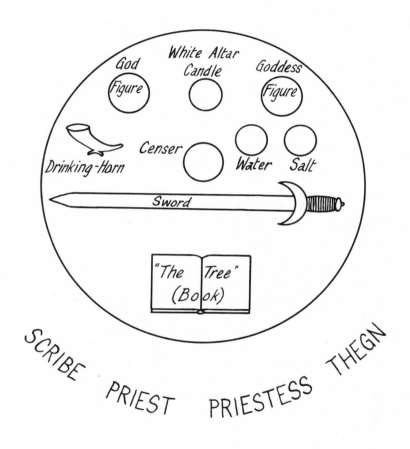

Layout of Seax-Wica Altar

position being unimportant. Most traditions have four such candles placed to mark the North, East, South and West points. The Saxons, however, use them purely for illumination. Some Saxon covens use seven candles (seven is a "magical" number) but any number may be used.

Standing before the Altar the Priest may be facing in any compass direction at all. He does not have to be facing specifically North, or East, or whatever. The Altar is not oriented in any special direction.

In addition to the tools on the Altar the individual Witches will each have a *Seax*, or short dagger (the equivalent to the *athame* of some other traditions). It should have a straight, double-edged, blade but other than that may be of any type. The handle may be of wood or bone (a "natural" substance is preferred) and may be of any color. There are no signs or symbols of any sort carved or written anywhere on the Seax.

The Witches themselves may be naked for their rites (many prefer this, for the sense of freedom, naturalness, equality, etc.) or, if preferred, may wear simple short tunics. These are white for the Priesthood; green, yellow, or brown—by personal preference—for the others. The tunics are sleeveless, of "miniskirt" length, and worn with a leather belt. Nothing is worn beneath the tunic. The neckline is cut in a "V", ofttimes to the waist. The feet are bare or sandalled. From the belt hangs the sheath for the Seax. When not in use the Seax is kept in this sheath (if the coven meets naked then a belt for the sheath might still be worn around the waist or, alternatively, the Seax might be laid on the ground at the Witch's feet).

Many of the *Seax-Wica* wear a copper or silver circlet about the head, and frequently a neck torque or talismanic pendant on a cord or chain. Rings, ofttimes with runic inscriptions, are also frequently worn.

The Sword is usually of Saxon design: flat and double-edged, approximately thirty inches in length and two-and-a-half inches wide. The cross-hilt may be straight but a crescent shape, curved towards the blade, is preferred. There are no signs or symbols carved or painted on the Sword.

Officers

Most Saxon covens appoint a *Scribe* and a *Thegn* (pronounced "Thain"), though these officers are not absolutely essential. The positions may be held by either male or female.

The SCRIBE's job is basically that of coven Secretary. He/she will handle any inter-coven correspondence (overseen by Priest or Priestess); advise coven members of meeting times and places; keep the minutes of the business meetings, and so on. At the back of *The Tree* is kept a list of the members of the Coven. A family-tree, in effect. The Scribe sees to it that names are entered here at Initiation; notations are made of Handfastings, Handpartings, etc. Should a person leave the coven for any reason (and anyone *may* leave at any time—no binding spells or curses exist!) or should a member die, then the Scribe will make the appropriate entry.

The Scribe is frequently chosen for his calligraphy. *The Tree* is always handwritten—never would it be typed.

The THEGN is part Guard, part Watchman, part Sergeant-at-Arms. He/she carries a Spear, a Hunting-horn, and (if available) a Shield, as symbols of the office. The Spear is approximately six feet in length, with a metal head. The Shield is wooden (sometimes covered with leather) and circular in shape. About two feet in diameter, it has a boss in the center and may be quite plain or elaborately decorated and/or studded. The Horn is slung from the shoulder and is blown to bring the people together (see the *Rites* below).

Ofttimes one member—not necessarily the same person at each meeting—will be given the task of ensuring that there is always incense burning in the censer, and of keeping an eye on the candles to see that they do not burn completely down.

During the rituals the Priest and Priestess stand before the Altar, Priest to the left of the Priestess. The Scribe stands left of the Priest and the Thegn to the right of the Priestess. The others then stand spread around the Circle.

The Book

The book contains all the rites, rituals, prayers, chants, etc., of the Coven. There is one main book used on the Altar. In this—usually at the back—is kept the "family-tree" of the Coven: the addition of new members, notations of death, or departure of old members, etc. The book is kept in the safe-keeping of the incumbent Priest and/or Priestess, and passed on to his/her successor. It is usually bound in green leather. The book is known as *The Tree* (the pages, of course, are the "leaves" of the Tree).

Individual Witches may also keep their own personal copies of *The Tree*, if they wish. In addition to the rites they might then also include notes of their personal interests: astrology, herbs, tarot, or whatever.

The Rites

The meeting-place is marked out by the Thegn. He uses the point of the Spear to scratch a circle on the ground around the centrally-located Altar. The circle is approximately nine feet in diameter (it does not have to be absolutely exact). This marking may be done before, after, or during the placing of the tools on the Altar. It is, therefore, simply a (physical) designating of the meeting area. The coven members may step over this line, into and out of the area, until the Thegn is asked to convene the Coven. This he does by blowing the Horn "to the four quarters" (North, East, South, and West). At this summoning all move into the Circle, greet one another,[1] and take up their positions thereabout.

---

[1] Where Witches of some traditions greet one another with the words "Blessed Be" or "Merry Meet; Merry Part", in the Saxon tradition Witches will always just kiss on meeting.

Erecting the Temple

[There should be wine, or ale, in the Drinking-Horns. The Priest[2] lights the Altar Candle and the Incense. The Priestess then takes the Altar Candle and moves *clockwise* around the Circle[3] lighting the Circle Candles from the Altar Candle, which she then replaces on the Altar.]

Thegn: "The Temple is about to be erected. Let all within this Temple be here of their own free will and accord, in Peace and in Love."

[Priestess takes her Seax and holds it with its point in the Salt, on the Altar.]

Priestess: "Salt is Life.[4] Let this Salt be pure and let it purify our lives, as we use it in these Rites, dedicated to Woden and to Freya."

---

[2] The Rites are written, throughout, as though both Priest and Priestess are present. If only one should be there, however, then that one plays both parts.

[3] You may generally walk in either direction around the Circle, unless the ritual specifically states one particular direction.

[4] See *The Symbolic Significance of Salt*, Ernest Jones.

[Priestess uses her Seax to lift three portions of the Salt and drop them into the Water. She then stirs the salted Water with the Seax, saying:]

Priestess: "Let the Sacred Salt drive out any impurities in this water that together they may be used in the service of Woden and of Freya; throughout these Rites and at any time and in any way we may use them."

[Priestess replaces Seax in its sheath, then taking up bowl of salted Water walks clockwise around the Circle sprinkling it along the marked boundary. She starts at any point, continuing around until the Circle is complete. She replaces the bowl on the Altar, then taking up the Censer again goes around, clockwise, censing the Circle. The Censer is then replaced on the Altar. Priest calls the male Witches, one by one, by name. At the call each moves to stand before the Priestess. She again takes up the dish of salted Water and, dipping in her fingers, marks a Pentagram (✩) on the Witch's chest.[5] Witch and Priestess then kiss.[6] When all males have been consecrated Priestess then calls the female Witches, one by one , by name. Priest consecrates them in the same manner.]

Priest: "Let us now invite the Gods to witness these Rites we hold in their honor."

[Priestess takes up Sword and holds it high. Holding their Seaxes high, all face the center of the Circle.]

Priestess: "Woden and Freya; God and Goddess; Father and Mother of all Life. Here do we invite you to join with us in our rites. Guard us and guide us within this Circle

---

[5] In some covens the genitals are also anointed. This practice dates from the days when fertility was important for man's existence.

[6] When there is only one Priest an embrace will suffice for members of the same sex.

and without it; in all things. So be it!"

All: "So be it!"

[All kiss the blade of their Seax; Priestess kisses Sword blade, then replaces it on the Altar. Others replace Seax in its sheath. Priest and Priestess each take a Drinking-Horn and spill a little of the ale on the ground[7] with the words:]

Priest &
Priestess: "Woden and Freya!"

[Priest and Priestess each take a drink then replace Horns on the Altar.]

Thegn: "Now is the Temple erected.
Let none leave it, but with good reason."

All: "So be it!"

*   *   *

Erecting the Temple *is done at the start of every meeting. It is, basically, the consecration of the meeting-place and of the participants. The purpose of the meeting—Esbat, Sabbat, or whatever—will continue from this point.*

---

[7] Should the meeting be taking place indoors then it is permissible to spill the libations into a Libation Dish, to be emptied onto the ground after the meeting.

Clearing the Temple

This ritual takes place at the end of every meeting.
[At the end of the meeting the Priestess will again raise the Sword high, and all will raise their Seaxes, as she says:]

Priestess: "We thank the Gods for their attendance. As we came together in love of them, and love of each other, so do we go our separate ways."

All: "Love is the Law, and Love is the Bond."

Thegn: "So be it! The Temple is now cleared."

[All kiss their blades and replace their Seaxes. They then move around the Circle to kiss one another in farewell.]

Self-Dedication

When you do not have access to an established Coven it is possible to Initiate yourself with the following simple ritual. If at some future date you come into contact with a coven (of the Seax-Wica*) then such an Initiation would be duly recognized.*

If a complete new group is starting then the chosen Priest and Priestess should each do the Rite of Self-Dedication. They can then Initiate the others of the group.

[The Ceorl[8] , who should always be naked for this rite, wearing no jewelry or clothing of any kind, Erects the Temple (anointing herself[9] with the salted Water). Ceorl kneels before the Altar and, with head bowed,

---

[8] Although no prior training may have been given this would-be Witch it is presumed that he/she will have some idea, at least, of the religion that is being entered. The term *Ceorl* is therefore used.

[9] The words *her, she*, etc., are used throughout this ritual to avoid the clumsiness of *he/she, his/her, she/him*, etc. The same ritual applies equally to both male and female.

42

meditates for three or four minutes on the God and the Goddess and the meaning of the Old Religion to her, the Ceorl. This is a final verification of her wish to dedicate herself.

Having satisfied herself that she is doing the right thing the Ceorl stands and lifts both arms high above the Altar.]

Ceorl: "Woden and Freya, hear me now!
          I am here a simple pagan[10] holding thee in
              honor.
          Far have I journeyed and long have I
              searched,
          Seeking that which I desire above all things.
          I am of the trees and of the fields.
          I am of the woods and of the springs;
          The streams and the hills.
          I am of thee; and thee of me."

[Lowers arms]
          "Grant me that which I desire.
          Permit me to worship the gods
          And all that the gods represent.
          Make me a Lover of Life in All Things.
          Well do I know the creed:
          That if I do not have that spark of Love
              within me,
          Then will I never find it without me.
          Love is the Law and Love is the Bond.
          All this do I honor above aught else."

[Ceorl takes up Seax in right hand,[11] kisses the blade, then holds it high.]

---

[10] The literal meaning of "pagan"—from the Latin *pagani*—is "one who dwells in the country". It is now used as a general term for a non-Christian and covers all traditions of Witchcraft.

[11] Left hand if left-handed.

43

"Woden and Freya, here do I stand before
   you,
Naked and unadorned, to dedicate myself
To thine honor.
Ever will I protect you and that which is
   yours.[1 2]
Let none speak ill of you, for ever
Will I defend you.
You are my life and I am yours
From this day forth.
So be it!"

[Ceorl again kisses the blade, then replaces Seax in sheath. She takes up the Drinking-Horn and slowly pours the remainder of the wine into the ground.]

   Ceorl: "As this wine (ale) drains from the Horn,
         So let the blood drain from my body
         Should I ever do aught to harm the Gods,
         Or those in kinship with their love.
         Woden and Freya!
         So be it!"

[Now a Gesith, she may meditate within the circle for as long as she will, or she may Clear the Temple at this point.

No other rituals should be done at this time. The Dedication should be done as a rite in itself—together with the Erecting and the Clearing of the Temple, of course.]

[1 2] All nature.

Initiation

If you finally locate a coven after *doing the Rite of Self-Dedication, no further initiation is necessary. Should you be accepted by the coven you would be accepted as a Gesith. If you make earlier contact with a coven, however, you will follow the path outlined above (HIERARCHY): Theow, Ceorl, Gesith. It is the path to be preferred, since it does include pre-coven training. This Initiation, by the Coven, is as follows:*

[The *Erecting the Temple* is performed in the usual manner. The Horned Helmet[13] is beside the Altar.

The Ceorl stands *outside* the Circle awaiting her summons. If the Coven normally wear tunics, then for the Initiation she alone is naked and wears no jewelry of any kind.]

Thegn: "Now is the Temple erected. Let none leave it but with good reason."

All: "So be it!"

[If the Ceorl is female the Priest now puts on the

---

[13] Worn by the Priest when representing the God. See footnote page 60. The helmet may be either horned *à la* Viking helmets, or may even be antlered.

Horned Helmet.]

Scribe: "Recorded in *The Tree* is the progress of one who would join us."

Priest: "What is her name?"

Scribe: "She is known as . . . (Name) . . ."[14]

Priestess: "What is her progress?"

Scribe: "Her Teacher must here advise."

Teacher: "As her Teacher do I speak. . . . (Name) . . .'s progress has been true.[15] She has Love in her heart."

Priestess: "Then should she join with us in the worship of the Mighty Ones. How say you all?"

All: "So be it!"

Thegn: ". . . (Name) . . . now stands without the Circle, prepared to enter this our Temple."

Priestess: "Then let her be brought before us."

[Thegn goes to the side of the Circle, by Ceorl, and sounds three notes on his horn. Ceorl walks into the Temple and moves to stand between the Priest and Priestess. Thegn draws his Spear along the line of the Circle, joining where it was "broken" by the Ceorl's passing. He remains standing there, facing inward.]

Priest: "I am he who speaks for Woden[16]. What is thy name?"

Ceorl: "I am known as . . . (Name) . . ."

Priest: "No more shall this be so."

[Priest removes Helmet and places it on the ground beside the Altar. He then takes the salted Water from the Altar and, dipping in his fingers, annoints the Ceorl

---

[14] Ceorl's everyday "given" name.

[15] Had the progress been "untrue" obviously the Initiation would not be taking place.

[16] For the Initiation of a *male* Ceorl the Priestess officiates, saying: "I am she who speaks for Freya. . . ."

on the forehead, breasts, and genitals, saying:]

Priest: "In the names of Woden and of Freya
          May this sacred water cleanse you.
          Let it drive out all impurities;
          All sadness and all hate."

[Priest replaces Water on the Altar, then kisses Ceorl fully on the lips.[17]]

Priest: "In the names of Woden and of Freya may
          you be filled with the Love that should be
          borne by and for all things."

[Ceorl kneels and Priest places his hands on her shoulders.]

Priest: "Now do I give you a new name. To your
          Brothers and Sisters of the Craft shall you
          be known henceforth as . . . (Name) . . .[18]
          You shall meet with us here in this Circle,
          or some other like spot, to worship Woden
          and Freya, and to learn and to love in their
          sight."

Ceorl: "So be it!"

[Priest kneels facing her and takes her hands in his.]

Priest: "What are the names of the Gods?"

Ceorl: "We know them as Woden and Freya."

Priest: "Are these the gods you wish to worship
          above all others?"

Ceorl: "They are."

Priest: "Do you promise faithfully to attend the

---

[17] In some covens the kiss is on the same points that were anointed.

[18] The "Witch Name" is here given as part of the *palingenesis,* or rebirth. This is the central theme of all such Initiations, Baptisms, puberty rites, etc. universally. Sometimes a symbolical death preludes the rebirth—hence the ritual scourging found in some Witch traditions. *cf Birth and Rebirth*, Mercea Eliade.

Ceorl:	Rites held in their honor, so far as you are able?"
Ceorl:	"I do."
Priest:	"Do you promise to defend them from those who would speak them ill?"
Ceorl:	"I do."
Priest:	"Do you promise to love and honor thy Brothers and Sisters of the Craft; to aid them when in distress; to care for them when sick; to protect and defend them from their enemies, so far as you are able?"
Ceorl:	"I do."
Priest:	"Know, then, that in all these things are we equal. In all things do we seek for the good of us all. Love is the Law, and Love is the Bond."
Ceorl:	"Love is the Law, and Love is the Bond."

[Both rise and kiss.]

Priest: "Now must you meet your kindred."

[Priest leads Ceorl around the Circle and introduces her, by her new name, to each Witch. Each one kisses her in greeting. Priestess is the last to greet her. Priest then takes the Drinking-Horn and slowly pours out the wine upon the ground.]

Priest: "As this wine (ale) drains from the Horn, so may the blood drain from your body should ever you do aught to harm the Gods, or those in kinship with their love. Woden and Freya! So be it!"

Ceorl: "So be it!"

[Priest replaces Horn on the Altar.]

Priestess: "Now are you a Gesith, and fully one of us."

[Priestess gives her a belt (and tunic, if worn by coven), which she puts on. Priest gives her a Seax. Others may give her jewelry, flowers, etc., if they so desire.]

Scribe: "As now a member of this Coven must I

ask you to place your name within *The Tree*."

[Gesith signs her Craft Name in the back of the book. Then shall follow the *Ceremony of the Cakes and Ale*, leading to general celebrations, before the *Clearing of the Temple*.]

Esbat

"Esbat" is the name given to a Craft general meeting other than one of the main festivals ("Sabbats").
[The *Erecting the Temple* is performed. Priest and Priestess kiss.]

Priest:	"Let us join in worship of Woden and Freya. Let us give thanks for all that we have; for the love we enjoy; for the kinship we share."
Priestess:	"Let us never forget what we owe to the Gods. For however our lives are shaped, they are so shaped by Our Lady and Her Lord. Theirs is the watch to keep; they are the ones who lead us on our paths."
Priest:	"It is right that we thank them for what we have. Yet also may we ask them for what we feel we need."
All:	"So be it!"

[Then follow three or four minutes of silence, while

---

[19] In Paganism, generally, it is thought far more efficacious to speak "from the heart" rather than read a set prayer, parrot-fashion, from a book.

each in his own way gives thanks or requests the help of the Gods.[19]]

Priestess: "When Man was but a child
Did the Gods watch over him.
Our loving Freya, the Goddess, was Man's
mother;
Whilst stern, strong, God Woden was his
father.
Man learned as he was taught,
With Patience and with Love.
Naught did he receive for naught.
But well was he rewarded for his pains.
'As ye give, so shall it return;'
And this he learned well.
Give of yourself, your love, your life;
And so will you gain immeasurably.
Take that which is not yours to take,
And you may find it not what it seemed.
The Gods are just and all they do with
reason.
Work well with them and you will be
rewarded
More than you might dream.
Our Lady is Love; Our Lord is Strength.
As we need them, they need us.
Let us live and love together
All in their sight.
Love is the Law, and Love is the Bond."

All: "So be it!"

[Then shall follow the *Ceremony of the Cakes and Ale.*]

Full Moon

Covens meet as frequently, or infrequently, as they wish; however, there should be no more than "one moontime" (one month) between meetings. If the coven meets weekly then the following ceremony is done at the meeting closest to the Full Moon, in lieu of that Esbat Ceremony. If the coven meets only once a month then the following ceremony is done in addition to the Esbat Ceremony (between it and the Cakes and Ale.)

[The *Erecting the Temple* is performed. Priest and Priestess kiss.]

Priest: "Now is the time when the Moon is full, signalling and lighting this night of our meeting. Let us call upon Woden and Freya to smile down upon us and pour forth their love."

[Priest and Priestess each raise their Seax high.]

Priest &
Priestess: "Woden and Freya!
We honor you; we love you!
All that you do
We know you do for our good.
So let all that we do
Be for the good of thee."

All: "So be it!"

[Priest lowers his Seax and, turning to face Priestess, kneels. She remains with Seax raised.]

Priest: "Lovely Lady Freya,
Known by so many names to so many Men,
At different times and different places—
Aphrodite, Bride, Cerridwen, Diana,
Arianrhod, Ea, Melusine, Isis[20] —
All these and many more
Were the names by which you were adored.
Yet do we know you as Freya,
And in that name is it meet that we
      worship you.
Adore we the spirit of you, and of your
      Lord,
In Love and in grateful thanks."

[Priestess lowers her Seax and raises Priest, kissing him. She then kneels to him.]

Priestess: "Woden, might God; our Lord!
All honor to thee, Consort of Freya.
Let us, your people, know you and love
      you.
Guard us well and guide us in our lives.
As Man needs Woman, so does Woman
      need Man.
So is it with the Gods.
Let us all be joined as one;
At one with the Gods."

All: "So be it!"

[Priest raises Priestess and they kiss. Then shall follow the *Ceremony of the Cakes and Ale.*]

---

[20] *cf* the "Charge" of Gardnerian and American-Celtic traditions.

Cakes and Ale

This ceremony is the "connecting-link" between the ritualistic part of a meeting and the working/social part—the sitting and talking on Craft or non-Craft matters; discussion of magick, healing, divination; consideration of personal, or coven, problems, etc. These things come after the worship. Honoring the Gods is first and foremost to the Seax-Wica.

Some Witch traditions have a similar ceremony called "Cakes and Wine". The fact that the Saxons call theirs "Cakes and Ale[21]*" is perhaps indicative of the "common" origins of the religion (the peasants and serfs would seldom, if ever, get to drink wine. Ale was their lot, and they were happy with it.) At coven-meetings today, however, many Witches do prefer to drink wine, though they retain the word "Ale" in the rites.*

This ceremony is not, and never was intended to be, a parody of the Christian Communion, for it far predates

---

[21] Ale is a fermented liquor similar to beer. The principle is extracted from several sorts of grain, most commonly from barley, after it has undergone the process of malting.

*that. It is found universally, in various forms, as a
thanking of the Gods for the necessities of life; thanking
them for the food and drink we need in order to live.*

[The Scribe takes the Drinking-Horns from the Altar
and, if empty, fills them with ale. He hands one to the
Priest and one to the Priestess. They raise them high.]

Priest: "As the Gods give to us, let us share with
them. And let us give thanks for all the
goodness they pour out upon the earth.
To the Gods!"

All: "To the Gods!"

[Priest and Priestess pour libations on the ground[22],
then take a drink from the horns. They then pass the
horns around the Circle and each person takes a drink.
The last to drink replace the horns on the Altar. The
Scribe then passes a plate of cakes[23] to the Priestess.
She holds the plate aloft.]

Priestess: "Our thanks to the Gods for the foods they
give us. Let us always see to it that aught
that we have we share, with those who have
nothing."

[Priestess offers cakes to Priest, who takes one. She
takes one herself then passes the plate around the Circle
for all.]

Priest: "Let us now sit and enjoy these gifts of the
Gods. But let us never forget that without
the Gods we would have nothing."

All: "So be it!"

[All now sit and individual drinking-horns, or goblets,
are filled and cakes distributed.

At this time will the Priest, or Priestess (or any who

---

[22] If the Circle should be held indoors then the libations may be
poured into a libation dish, to be emptied onto the ground
later.

[23] Cakes, cookies, biscuits, or anything representative.

55

requests to do so), speak out on any matters of importance[24]. Then will there be general talk till the *Clearing the Temple*.]

[24] In effect a sermon, though open to question/discussion by all, if necessary.

Sabbats

There are eight Sabbats in the year: four major ones *(Samhain, Imbolc, Beltane, Lughnasadh),* and four minor ones *(Spring and Autumn Equinox, Summer and Winter Solstice).*

Margaret Murray points out *("God of the Witches", 1931)* that the two most important—Samhain and Beltane—coincide with the breeding seasons of both wild and domestic animals. These Pagan festivals were later exploited by the Christian Church *(Imbolc = Candlemas; Lugnasadh = Lammas,etc.)* In the early days of Christianity Pope Gregory the Great realized that since these were the times people were accustomed to come together for worship it would behoove the Church to establish the Christian festivals on these same dates.

Note: *The* Erecting the Temple *is performed as a prelude to all other rites, including the Sabbats. Should a Full Moon coincide with a Sabbat date, the* Full Moon *ritual is performed immediately following the* Erecting the Temple, *and is then followed by the Sabbat ritual.*

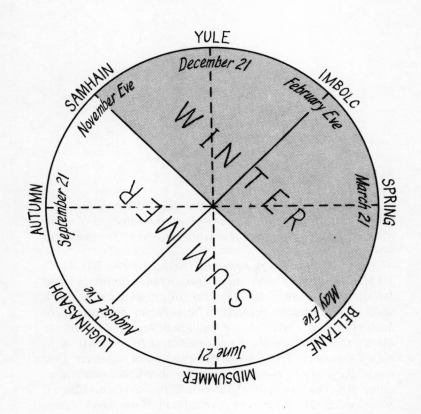

YULE
December 21

IMBOLC
February Eve

SAMHAIN
November Eve

WINTER

SPRING
March 21

AUTUMN
September 21

SUMMER

BELTANE
May Eve

LUGHNASADH
August Eve

MIDSUMMER
June 21

Pagan "Wheel" of the Year

Samhain Sabbat

Samhain is the old name for All Hallow's Eve, or Hallowe'en. It originally marked the change of season from summer to winter, together with the shift of emphasis from the (summer) Goddess—overlooking the crops—to the (winter) God—overlooking the hunt.

[The outer edge of the Circle may be decorated with autumnal flowers, branches, pine-cones, small pumpkins, etc.. There may also be flowers on the Altar. On the Altar (or on the ground beside it, if there is insufficient room) rests the Priest's Horned Helmet.]

Priestess: "As Goddess-Summer draws to a close
So begin the dark months of the God-Winter.
All praise be to Freya, and to Woden her Consort."

All: "All praise!"

Priestess (raising Seax):
"Gracious Goddess, we thank you
For the joys of Summer;
For the crops, the harvest;
For life, for love.
We, who love you, as we know you love us.
Return again next year, when your time is

come.
When your companion-love, our Lord,
Has led us safely through the dark.
We love you and honor you
Freya, most beautiful."
All: "Love!"
[Priestess puts Seax in its sheath then takes up
Horned Helmet and holds it high.]
Priestess: "Here do I hold the symbol[25]
Of Woden the Mighty One,
Lord of Life and of Death.
As he will guard us and guide us
Through the months to come,
So will his servant, our Priest, here."
[She places Horned Helmet on Priest's head.]
"Now do you, . . . (Priest's Name) . . .
represent Woden.
For him you speak; for him you act.
Lead us, we ask you, through the hardships
That lie ahead, that again we may see
The glory of spring, and the love
Of our Lady Freya."
[They kiss]
Priest: "As Lord of Life, of Love, of Death,
Would Lord Woden bid you have no fear.
So be it!
With my lady at my side
I shall know always there is light.
I shall know always there is hope of life to
come.
I will lead you happily as I lead those

---

[25] From the Palaeolithic origins of the God, as a God of Hunting,
he is frequently thought of as a horned deity. This was
because most of the animals hunted, in early times, were
horned. (*cf God of the Witches*, Murray; *Witchcraft From the
Inside*, Buckland).

Who have gone before, yet are here now.
So be it!"

All: "So be it!"

[Priest and Priestess kiss. Priestess leads others around Circle, as Priest stands facing out from the Altar. Each male embraces the Priest; each female kisses him. When all are back to their places Priest replaces Horned Helmet on the Altar.]

Priest: "Now is the time for celebration, to give us strength, to give us joy. Our loved ones return from Drēun[26] to join with us. Let us greet them, and one another. Let us feast and make merry. Let us remember those who have gone on to the domains of the Mighty Ones. That they may return briefly to revel with us is good.[27] This night is for merriment 'ere the hardships of winter enfold us. Be happy all. So be it!"

All: "So be it!"

[Then shall follow the *Ceremony of Cakes and Ale* followed by games and merriment.]

[26] In many traditions known as the Summerland. This is the one place where everyone goes at death—no separate "Heaven" and "Hell". Witches believe that those who have died, who were near and dear will return to celebrate with them at Samhain. This is one reason this time of year is especially associated with ghosts .

[27] Witches do not "call Back" the dead. They do not hold *séances*—such belongs to Spiritualism. They do, however, believe that *if the dead themselves wish it* they will return at the Sabbat to share in the love and celebration of the occasion.

Yule Sabbat

[The *Erecting the Temple* is performed, Priest and Priestess kiss. On the Altar stand two unlit candles, one on either side of the Altar Candle.]

Priestess: "Now is the sun well on its course
Through the long dark months of winter."

Priest: "Let us show our love for the Gods
By sending strength where it is needed.
Let us kindle here fresh fires
To light our Lord upon his way.
Fires to give him confidence;
To show him our love burns forth
Even though the hardships of winter be
upon us."

All: "So be it!"

Priest takes up one of the unlit candles and holds it before him.]

Priest: "Let Woden bear the blessings of our Lady
Freya
As he guards us and guides us
Through the long dark days ahead.
May all our power, Wiccans all,
Be symbolised by this light,
As it burns with steady flame,

Aiding and strengthening that which is
there."

[He lights his candle from the Altar Candle and
stands it alongside. Priestess takes up other unlit
candle.]

Priestess: "To that do we add a further prayer.
One light to take him into the winter,
Yet another light to lead him back.
That my Lady Freya be ever with my Lord
Woden
Is meet and right, and be it so.
Let our prayers and thoughts go with him
For as he guards and guides us
So do we love him,
And so have we trust in all things."

[Priestess lights candle from Altar Candle and stands
it alongside.]

Priest &
Priestess: "Let these lights burn
Till Imbolc time,
When we shall know
The worst of winter is behind us."

All: "So be it!"

Priest: "And so here be the love
Of the God for the Goddess."

[Priest kisses Priestess. Then shall follow the *Ceremony of Cakes and Ale*, followed by games and
merriment.]

Imbolc Sabbat

The *Erecting the Temple* is performed. Priest and
Priestess kiss. On the Altar stand the two additional
candles added at Yule. They are alight. Each Witch has
an unlit candle tucked into his/her belt.]
Priestess: "Now has the Lord reached the zenith
Of his journey.
It is meet that we rejoice for him.
From now till Beltane is the path ahead less
dark,
For he can see the Lady at its end."
Priest: "I urge ye, Wiccans all,
To give now your hearts to our Lord
Woden.
Let us make this a Feast of Torches
To carry him forward, in light,
To the arms of Freya."
[Priest and Priestess take up the two extra candles.
Witches take their candles from their belts.]
Priest &
Priestess: "Light now your flames from the Sacred
Altar."
[All females light their candles from the Priest's; all
males light from the Priestess's. When all are lit they are

held up high in the air in the left hand, Seaxes high in the right.[28]]

    All: "To Woden, the Mighty One,
                Do we give our love and our strength.
                So be it!"

[All hold for a few moments, till the Priest and Priestess give the signal. Then each kisses the blade of her Seax, blows out her candle—except for Priest and Priestess, who replace theirs, still lit, on the Altar—and puts away her Seax.]

    Priest: "Thus shall the journey be made through to Beltane, renewed in Strength and happy in Love."

    Priestess: "As the Gods give to us, so is it right that we should give to the Gods."

    All: "So be it!"

[Then shall follow the *Ceremony of Cakes and Ale* followed by games and merriment.]

---

[28] A left-handed person would hold Seax in left hand, candle in right.

Spring Sabbat

[The *Erecting the Temple* is performed. Priest and Priestess kiss. Let there be spring flowers on the Altar and about the Circle. On the Altar, beside the Sword, rests a Priapic, or pine-tipped, Wand. Also on the Altar is a small bowl filled with fresh soil and, beside it, a large seed of some sort.]

Priest: "Seax-Wica, harken to me!
Awake! It is time to greet the Spring.
Freya, Lady of Light, hear us!
Woden, Lord of Life, hear us!
We are here to celebrate both with you and
for you."

[Priestess raises both arms high.]

Priestess   "Welcome, welcome, beauteous Spring!
Now let us join together, inspired by the
Gods.
Let us cast behind us the darkness of
Winter,
And look again forward to that which lies
ahead.
Now is the time for birth.
Now is the time for the planting of seeds."

[Priestess lowers her arms. Priest takes up the Priapic

66

Wand and holds it out, vertically, before him.]

Priestess: "By the power of the raised Wand
Doth the Seed find the Furrow.
Blessings be upon this handsome Wand.

[Priest turns to face her. She kisses the tip of the Wand.]

All honor to it;
May it be ever thus."

All: "All power to the Wand,
All power!
For Love is here.
Blessed be!"

[Priest and Priestess lead a dance about the Altar, Priest carrying the Priapic Wand. All sing[29] as they dance. When they have danced sufficiently they stop. Priest replaces Wand on Altar and the Priestess takes up the bowl of earth.]

Priestess: "Of old would we celebrate by together planting
The seed, one with another,
Yet here do we symbolize that act,
In veneration of our Lady and our Lord."

[Priestess turns to face Priest and holds bowl close between her breasts. Priest takes his Seax and carefully makes a depression in the soil, in the center of the bowl. Putting away his Seax he then takes up the seed, from the Altar, and holds it cupped in his hands over the bowl.]

Priest: "These rites of Spring belong to all;
To us and to the Gods.
This is a joyous time.
This is a time for planting."

[He places the seed in the depression in the soil and covers it with earth.]

[29] See Appendix B for songs used by the Old Religion.

"This seed I do place in the womb of the
            Earth,
That it may become a part of the Earth;
A part of Life,
A part of us.
Blessed are the Gods!
Blessed are the Seax-Wica!
Let Love abound!"

All: "Love! So be it!"

[Priest and Priestess kiss, then the Priestess replaces
the bowl on the Altar. All kiss one another.

Then shall follow the *Ceremony of Cakes and Ale,*
followed by games and merriment.]

Beltane Sabbat

[The *Erecting the Temple* is performed. Priest and Priestess kiss. There should be spring flowers spread about the Circle and on the Altar. Also on the Altar rests a crown of flowers, ready for the Priestess. To one side of the Circle—perhaps behind the Altar—stands a cauldron filled with kindling.]

Priestess: "With this night do we see
The ending of the Dark Time.
Our Lord Woden has passed through
To bring us once more to the light,
And to our Lady Freya."

All: "Woden! Our thanks and our love to thee!"

[Scribe lights the kindling in the cauldron.]

Priest: "Now light we the Beltane fires!
To revitalize our Lord
After his long journey.
Welcome Woden!
Welcome Life!"

All: "Welcome Woden! Welcome Life!"

[All now dance around the Circle, jumping over the flaming cauldron, if they wish. They dance either singly or in couples, as they wish. Priestess remains at the Altar. While the Witches dance she says:]

Priestess: "The Year is a mighty wheel
And the Sabbats are its spokes;
As this Circle is also a wheel
Made up of we Wiccan folks.
Ahead now lies the Sun—
Lord Woden still shining down[30] —
Whilst our Lady has begun
To spread her Springtime gown.
With bud and twig and leaf and tree,
We welcome Freya so merrily."

[Priest alone stops dancing and says:]

Priest: "Welcome indeed to our Lady fair.
Welcome, thrice welcome, we fill the air
With our love and devotion for Freya!"

[When others have stopped dancing Priest continues:]

"As our Lord Woden steps back
So does our Lady Freya move forward,
To guard us and guide us
Through the Summer time.

[He takes up the crown of flowers.]

Let these flowers be my Lady's crown,
As our beloved Priestess . . . (Name) . . .
Wears them proudly."

[Priestess kneels and Priest places crown on her head.[31] He then raises her and kisses her. All then move round the Circle to kiss the Priestess and say "Love".]

Priestess: "The word is 'Love' and happily do we say
it;
The word is 'Love' and merrily do we make

---

[30] This is not to say that the Seax-Wica worship the sun, merely that they look upon it as a symbol for Woden, their God.

[31] Should there be no Priestess then the crown may be placed on the head of any female chosen. If there should be no females then it is placed on the Altar.

it;
The word is 'Love' and fully do we feel it;
For we *are* Love."
[Then shall follow the *Ceremony of Cakes and Ale,*
followed by games and merriment.]

Midsummer Sabbat

[The *Erecting the Temple* is performed. Priest and
Priestess kiss.]
Priestess: "Now is the summer sun on high,
                Yet living goes ever on.
                With hope in our hearts   ⬦
                Let us spread happiness about us.
                Cease all sorrows!
                Cease all strife!
                The day is for living—
                For living this life!"
Priest: "On high the sun casts never a shadow.
                So shines down the love of the Gods—
                Of Woden and Freya—
                Shining upon us all alike.
                No more on one than on another."
Priestess: "As the sun moves on its path,
                Acknowledging all along its way;
                So move we for the Mighty Ones,
                To show our love and affection."
[Priest and Priestess then move, hand-in-hand,
clockwise about the Circle kissing each Witch[32] along

---

[32] Priest kisses females; Priestess kisses males.

the way. Returning to their original positions they kiss each other.]

Priestess: "We Wiccans give thanks to the Mighty Ones,
To Woden and to Freya,
For the richness and goodness of life.
As there must be rain with the sun,
To make all things good;
So must we suffer pain with our joy,
To know all things.
Our love is ever with the Gods,
For though we know not their thoughts
Yet do we know their hearts—
That all is for our good.
Woden and Freya, bless us now.
Keep us faithful in thy service.
We thank you for the crops;
For life, for love, for joy.
We thank you for that spark
That brings us together—and to you.
Help us to live with Love
And with Trust between us.
Help us to feel the joy of loving you
And of loving one another."

All: "So be it!"

[Then shall follow the *Ceremony of Cakes and Ale,* followed by games and merriment.]

Lughnasadh Sabbat

[The *Erecting the Temple* is performed. Priest and Priestess kiss.]

Priest: "Summer is the season for cultivation and
     for caring.

     Flowers come forth; later to give way to
     fruit.

     Now is the time for us to review all things—

     That which is to remain, and that which
     must

     Be pruned away, for the goodness of
     growth.

     Growth in all things; in plants and in
     ourselves."

Priestess (Raising her arms high):

     "Almighty Mother of us all,

     Bringer of Life and of Love,

     We thank thee for all the goodness

     We have raised up from the soil;

     The promises of fruits to come.

     Help us in our decisions and in our
     judgements.

     Let us have the wisdom of the Mighty Ones

     As we handle our problems

74

Both great and small."

All: "So be it!"

[Priestess lowers her arms.]

Priest: "My Lady of the Silver Crescent—
And the Golden Orb, your Consort—
We praise you and love you.
Look down upon us and guide us
In our rites and in our lives."

Priestess: "As the Moon reflects the Sun
So let our lives reflect the love you have for
us.
Help us to love and honor one another;
To have respect and, most of all,
To have that understanding that brings
True love and peace.
Woden and Freya, we pagan folks are
yours;
In love most perfect
And with trust in all things."

[Priest and Priestess kiss, then lead a dance about the Circle. All dance till the Priestess signals a stop. Then shall follow the *Ceremony of Cakes and Ale,* followed by games and merriment.]

Autumn Sabbat

[The *Erecting the Temple* is performed. Priest and Priestess kiss. Let there be autumnal flowers on the Altar and about the Circle—pine cones, leaves, and boughs.]

Scribe: "Now that the season of plenty draws to its close
Let us listen to the words of Freya,
As she speaks through her Priestess . . .
(Name) . . . here."

[Priestess spreads her hands toward the people.]

Priestess: "My love is ever with my Saxon Pagans.
Although the season of plenty draws to a close
Think not that I forsake you,
For I am with you always.
I watch over you, as does my Consort, the Hornéd One.
When the dark months descend
Then will Woden hold vigil over you;
As will you over him.
For know you that as Man needs the Gods

So do the Gods need Man[33] ."

[Priestess lowers her arms and takes up from the Altar the bowl of Salted Water. Priest leads Witches in a dance about the Circle, the Priestess sprinkling them with the water as they pass. They dance around three times. Priestess replaces bowl.]

Priestess: "To the good seasons that have already passed,
And to those that are yet to come."

All: "Woden and Freya give blessings."

Priest: "To the beauty of autumn,
And to those good friends we treasure."

All: "Woden and Freya give blessings."

Priestess: "To Woden and Freya,
Who bring peace, joy, and love to the world."

All: "Do we give our blessings."

Priest &
Priestess: "So be it!"

[Then shall follow the *Ceremony of Cakes and Ale,* followed by games and merriment.]

[33] Witchcraft, in company with most of the older religions, does not hold that the gods are omnipotent and omniscient. They are much more "human" and need Man as much as Man needs the gods. They also may have their good moods, or their bad moods. For this reason Witches do not believe in (nor, of course, worship) the Devil, the concept of such a figure being dependant upon an all-good deity.

Hand-Fasting[34]

This rite is best performed during the waxing of the Moon[35]. The Altar may be decked with flowers, and flowers strewn about the Circle. If the Coven normally wears tunics, for the Hand-Fasting the Bride and Groom should be naked.

It is traditional, in the Seax-Wica, for the Bride and Groom to exchange rings. These are usually silver bands with the couple's (Craft) names inscribed on each of them in Runes (see under Woden *above). These rings rest on the Altar at the start of the rite.*

[The *Erecting the Temple* is performed. Priest and Priestess kiss.]

> *Thegn:* "There are those in our midst who seek the bond of Handfasting."
>
> *Priestess:* "Let them be named and brought forward."
>
> *Scribe:* "... (Groom's Name) ... is the Man, and

---

[34] Wedding ceremony of the Seax-Wica.

[35] During the *increase* of the Moon—after the New Moon; approaching the Full Moon.

. . . (Bride's Name) . . . is the Woman."

[Bride and Groom come forward to stand facing Priest and Priestess across the Altar—Bride before Priest and Groom before Priestess.]

Priestess (to Groom):
   ·"Are you . . . (Name) . . . ?"
Groom: "I am."
Priestess: "And what is your desire?"
Groom: "To be made one with . . . (Bride's Name) . . . in the eyes of the Gods and of the Seax-Wica."

Priest (to Bride):
   "Are you . . . (Name) . . . ?"
Bride: "I am."
Priest: "And what is your desire?"
Bride: "To be made one with . . . (Groom's Name) . . . , in the eyes of the Gods and of the Seax-Wica."

[Priestess takes up Sword and raises it high.]

Priestess: "Freya and Woden, here before you stand two of your folk. Witness, now, that which they have to declare."

[Priestess replaces Sword on Altar; takes her Seax and holds the point of it to Groom's chest.]

Priestess: "Repeat after me: 'I, . . . (Name) . . . ,[36] do come here of my own free will, to seek the Partnership of . . . (Bride's Name) . . . . I come with all love, honor, and sincerity, wishing only to become One with her whom I love. Always will I strive for . . . (Bride's Name) . . .'s happiness and welfare. Her life will I defend before my own. May the Seax be plunged into my heart should I not be sincere in all that I declare. All this I swear in the names of Freya and Woden.

[36] Groom repeats Oath, line by line.

79

May they give me the strength to keep my vows. So be it!' "

[Priestess lowers her Seax. Priest then raises his Seax and, in turn, holds it to the breast of the Bride.]

Priest: "Repeat after me: 'I, ... (Name) ..., do come here of my own free will, to seek the Partnership of ... (Groom's Name). ... I come with all love, honor, and sincerity, wishing only to become One with him whom I love. Always will I strive for ... (Groom's Name) ...'s happiness and welfare. His life will I defend before my own. May the Seax be plunged into my heart should I not be sincere in all that I declare. All this I swear in the names of Freya and Woden. May they give me the strength to keep my vows. So be it!'"

[Priest lowers the Seax. Priestess takes up the two rings and sprinkles and censes both[37]. She then hands the Bride's ring to the Groom and the Groom's ring to the Bride.]

Priest: "As the grass of the fields and the trees of the woods bend together under the pressures of the storm, so too must you both bend when the wind blows strong. But know that as quickly as the storm comes, so equally quickly may it leave. Yet will you both stand, strong in each other's strength. As you give love; so will you receive love. As you give strength; so will you receive strength. Together you are one; apart you are as nothing."

Priestess: "Know you that no two people can be

---

[37] She dips her fingers into the salted water and sprinkles it on the rings. She then holds them both, for a moment, in the smoke of the incense.

exactly alike; no more can any two people fit together, perfect in every way. There will be times when it will seem hard to give and to love. But see then your reflection as in a woodland pool: When the image you see looks sad or angered, Then is the time for you to smile and to love, (for it is not fire that puts out fire). In return will the image in the pool smile and love. So change you anger for love, and tears for joy. It is no weakness to admit a wrong; more is it a strength and a sign of learning."

Priest: "Ever love, help, and respect each other,
And then know truly that you are One
In the eyes of the Gods,
And of the Seax-Wica."

All: "So be it!"

[Bride and Groom each place ring on other's finger and kiss. They then kiss Priest and Priestess across the Altar and move about the Circle to be congratulated by the others.

Then shall follow the *Ceremony of Cakes and Ale,* followed by games and merriment.]

Hand-Parting

In many religions marriage is meant to be a lifetime partnership. Hence, though it may turn out that after a few years, or however long, a couple are really unsuited for one another, they are "stuck" for the rest of their lives. This invariably leads to incredible unhappiness— perhaps even eventual hatred—for husband, wife, and any children of the marriage. Although Witches most certainly do not encourage "casual" partnerships they do recognise the fact that some marriages just do not work out ideally. When this is the case—and all attempts have been made to settle any differences—then they will dissolve the partnership with the old ceremony of Hand-Parting. This is never, of course, undertaken lightly.

Before the Ceremony the Couple will sit with the Priest and Priestess and work out a fair division of their property, plus provision for support of any children of the marriage. The Scribe will make note of this, and the record will be signed by all. If either Husband or Wife are not available for the rite (by reason of re-location, ill health, or whatever) then a Witch of the appropriate sex will stand in for the missing party. The rite will take place in this fashion *only* if there is a signed agreement received from the missing party, together with the ring (see rite below).

[The *Erecting the Temple* is performed. Priest and Priestess kiss.]

Thegn: "... (Husband's Name) ... and ... (Wife's Name) ... stand forth!"

[Husband and Wife stand before the Altar, facing Priest and Priestess across it: Husband before Priestess, Wife before Priest.]

Priestess: "Why are you here?"

Husband: "I wish a Handparting from ... (Name) ..."

Priest: "Why are you here?"

Wife: "I wish a Handparting from ... (Name) ..."

Priestess: "Do you both desire this of your own free will?"

Husband & Wife: "We do."

Priest: "Has a settlement been reached between you regarding division of property, and (*if appropriate*) care for the child(ren)?"

Husband & Wife: "It has."

Priest: "Has this been duly recorded, signed, and witnessed?"

Scribe: "It has."

Priest: "Then let us proceed, remembering that we stand ever before the Gods."

[Husband and Wife join hands.]

Priestess: "Together, repeat after me: 'I, ... (Name[38]) ..., do hereby most freely dissolve my partnership with ... (Spouse's Name). ... I do so in all honesty and sincerity, before Woden and Freya, with

---

[38] Husband and Wife speak together.

83

my Brothers and Sisters of the Seax-Wica as witnesses. No longer are we as One; but are now two Individuals, free to go our separate ways. We release all ties, one to the other, yet ever will we retain respect for one another, as we have love and respect for our fellow Wiccans. So be it!' "

Priest: "Hand-Part!"

[Husband and Wife release each others hands, remove their wedding bands and give them to the Priestess. She sprinkles and censes them, saying:]

Priestess: "In the names of Woden and Freya do I cleanse these rings."

[She returns them to the couple, to do with them as they wish.]

Priestess: "Now are you Handparted. Let all know you as such. Go your separate ways in Peace and in Love—never in bitterness—and in the ways of the Craft. So be it!"

All: "So be it!"

[Then shall follow the *Ceremony of Cakes and Ale* and *Clearing the Temple.]*

Birth Rite

Witches, generally speaking, are very open-minded people, especially where religion is concerned. Most traditions, including the Seax-Wica, have no hard and fast Commandments; no catechisms. They feel that all should be free to choose the religion that best suits them. It would seem obvious that there can be no one religion for all. Temperaments differ. Some love ritual for its own sake; others look for simplicity. Most religions lead in the same direction, simply taking different paths to get there. Witches feel all should therefore be free to choose their own paths. All—including the Witches' own children. A child should not be forced to follow a particular religion just because it is the religion of the parent. For this reason most Witch parents try to give their children as wide a view of religion as possible, that the child may make a free choice when ready. It is naturally hoped that the child will choose the Craft, but it is not forced. Far better that she be happy in a religion different from the parent, than that she become a religious hypocrite.

For the above reasons there is no Craft "baptism" in the Seax-Wica. In the simple ceremony below the parents ask the Gods to watch over the child and give it *wisdom in its choice, when it is older. The child actually will be Initiated only when she is old enough to decide for herself (exact age will, of course, vary from child to child). Until that time she certainly may attend meetings as a* Ceorl. *When the child feels ready the Initiation generally will be conducted by the Priest and Priestess, but, if they so wish, the parents may take those parts for the rite.*

(As with virtually all branches of the Craft anyone may leave the Seax-Wica at any time, should they so wish. There would be no dire curse following them! Similarly, if they do leave they are free to return again, after any length of time, should they so desire. They would not, then, need to go through another Initiation.)

This rite may be performed at any of the rituals, prior to the Ceremony of Cakes and Ale, *or it may be done as a rite in itself, preceded by* Erecting the Temple *and followed by the* Ceremony of Cakes and Ale *and, of course,* Clearing the Temple.

[The *Erecting the Temple* is performed. Priest and Priestess kiss.]

Scribe:　"There is an addition to our number.
　　　　　Let us give him/her due welcome."

[Parents move to stand across the Altar from the Priest and Priestess. They hold the baby[39].]

Priest:　"What is the name of the child?"

[Parents give the child's name—the name by which it will be known in the Circle until old enough to choose its own name.]

Priest:　"We welcome you, . . . (Name) . . ."

Priestess: "Welcome, and much love to you."

[Priestess dips her fingers in the Salted Water and gently wipes them over the baby's face. Mother then

---

[39] As they have done throughout the *Erecting the Temple*.

passes the child through the smoke of the incense.[40]]

Priestess: "May our Lady Freya and her Consort
Woden
Smile ever upon you.
May they guard you and guide you through
this life.
May they help you choose that which is
right
And shun that which is wrong;
That no harm may befall you,
Or others through you.
So be it!"

All:　　"Welcome!"

[Then shall follow the Ceremony of Cakes and Ale.]

[40] In effect the child has been "sprinkled and censed", i.e. cleansed of all impurity.

Crossing the Bridge (At Death)

Since the Seax-Wica, in company with other traditions, believe in reincarnation, death is a time for celebration rather than grief. Death signifies the completion of a learning period—the individual has "graduated" and will be going on to other things. This, they feel, should be celebrated. Sorrow, then, is a sign of selfishness. We are sorry for ourselves, that we have been left behind without the love and company of one dear to us.

As with other aspects of the religion there are no hard and fast teachings on what should be done with the body at death. It was but a shell for the spirit, or soul, that inhabited it and has now gone on (see Reincarnation above).

This rite may be performed at any of the other rituals, prior to the *Ceremony of Cakes and Ale,* or it may be done as a rite in itself, preceded by *Erecting the Temple* and followed by the *Ceremony of Cakes and Ale* and, of course, *Clearing the Temple.*

[The Erecting the Temple is performed. Priest and Priestess kiss. Thegn sounds a long note on the Horn.]

Thegn: "The Horn is sounded for . . . (Name of Dead Witch) . . ."

88

All: "So be it!"

Priestess: "That today . . . (Name) . . . is not with us, here in the Circle, saddens all. Yet let us try *not* to feel sad. For is this not a sign that he/she has fulfilled this life's work? Now is he/she free to move on. We shall meet again, fear not. And that will be a time for further celebration."

Priest: "Let us send forth our good wishes to bear him/her over the Bridge.[41] May he/she return at any time to be with us here."

[All take their Seaxes and point them at a spot behind the Altar, facing the Priest and Priestess. They imagine the dead Witch standing in that spot, looking as they best remember him/her. They concentrate on sending Love, Joy, Happiness, from their bodies, along the line of the Seax, into the imagined body. This continues for a few moments. The Priestess signals the end by replacing her Seax and saying:]

Priestess: "We wish you all the Love and Happiness we may.

We will never forget you:

Do not you forget us.

Whenever we meet here, you are always welcome."

All: "So be it!"

[All now sit, and if any present wish to speak of the dead they may do so. If no one else, then at least the

---

[41] As the Romans believed themselves ferried across the River Styx by the ferryman Charon to Hades, their land of the after-life, so the Seax-Wica believe themselves to cross a (perhaps metaphorical) Bridge to Drëun. They send forth their "wishes," i.e. "power", not because the dead could not cross without it, but to let the dead know that they are not forgotten.

Priest or Priestess should speak reminiscently of the dead Gesith. Then shall follow the *Ceremony of Cakes and Ale*.]

Consecration

It is considered "proper" to consecrate the two main tools used in the rites: the Seax and the Sword. This consecration is, basically, a spiritual cleansing of the instrument. It is accomplished through "sprinkling (with the salted water) and censing (in the smoke of the incense)". It is done once only. The Sword would be done when the coven is first formed; the Seax when the Witch first becomes a Gesith. It is not, therefore, necessary to repeat this consecration before every meeting.

[Gesith moves to stand between Priest and Priestess—if *Sword* is to be consecrated this is done by the Priestess. Gesith raises Seax high, as though in salute.]

Gesith: "Mighty Woden and Lovely Freya,
Here is my Seax (Sword),
A weapon in thine honor.
Purify it for me,
And help me to keep it pure in thy service.[42] "

[42] In many traditions the ritual knife, or *Athame* as it is sometimes called, may not be used outside the Circle. It is considered a purely ritual instrument. With the Saxons, however, the Seax may be used at any time. The more it is used by its owner the more *mana* (power) it acquires.

[Gesith places the Seax on the Altar, between the Sword and the Censer. Dipping her fingers in the Salted Water she sprinkles the Seax; turns it over and sprinkles the other side. She then picks it up and passes it slowly through the smoke of the incense. She again raises it high.]

Gesith: "Again here is my weapon.
Symbolically have I washed away
Aught that is evil.
I have covered it with the all-encompassing
    incense
Of all that is good.
Let it always be pure in thy service.
And let it keep and guard me
From all harm,
In all things wherein I shall use it.
So be it, in the names of Woden and
    Freya."

All: "So be it!"

This ritual can be adapted for many things. Should someone wish to consecrate a talisman ("good luck piece"), love token, or similar, the above ritual may be followed. The wording should be added to or adapted to make it appropriate to the article being consecrated, of course.

Galdra (Magick)

Magick is a practice. Hence, anyone may do magick—or, at least, *attempt* to do it. Magick done for Good purposes is labelled White Magick; for Evil purposes, Black Magick. These terms come from the early Persian concepts of Good and Evil. Zoroaster (Zarathustra) decided that of all the many, hitherto basically good, spirits, or *devi*, there was actually only one who was *all*-good. This was Ahura-Mazda—the Sun, the Light. If you have an all-good deity then you have to have an all-evil opposite (you cannot have "white" unless you have "black" as a contrast), so the role was given to Ahriman—the Darkness. The other minor *devi* became "devils". This concept of all-good/all-bad was picked up later in Mithraism and moved west into Christianity. So from Persia do we get the basic ideas for "White" Magick and "Black" Magick.

Since anyone can do Magick there can be White Magicians and Black Magicians—those trying to help others and those trying to harm. By virtue of the Seax-Wica's belief in retribution, however, you *cannot* have a so-called "Black Witch". It would be a contradiction in terms.

Galdra is the Saxon for "Magick".

A *Galdorcraeftig* is "a person proficient in magick".

Below are a few examples of the (White) Magick that would be done by a Seax-Wican.

Protection From Evil

There is no actual Rite of Protection in Saxon Witchcraft. If a Coven felt that someone or something malevolent was directing evil toward them they would know that the very Circle in which they stood was ample protection. For an individual Gesith the very holding of the Seax (and, if necessary, using the Seax to draw a Circle about her) would be a protection.

However, if for any reason it was felt that someone might be directing evil—perhaps over a period of time—then a witch would almost certainly make what is known as a "Witch's Bottle". This is an old defense known, throughout folklore, to Witches and non-Witches alike. The idea is to protect yourself and, at the same time, send *back* whatever is being sent to you. You should never be the originator of evil (*see Retribution above*), but you may certainly protect yourself.

To make a Witch's Bottle use a regular jar, such as a small (6oz.) "instant" coffee type of jar. Half fill the jar with sharp objects—broken glass, old razor-blades, rusty nails, screws, pins, needles, etc. When the jar is half-full of these objects, urinate in it to fill it.[1] (If a woman is

[1] Urine features in many an old folk charm. See, for example, Vance Randolph's *Ozark Superstitions* (Dover, N.Y. 1964).

preparing the bottle she should endeavor to get a little menstrual blood into it as well). Put the top on the jar and seal it. It should be buried in the ground at least twelve inches deep, and preferably in an isolated spot where it may remain undisturbed.

So long as the bottle remains buried and unbroken it will protect you from any evil directed knowingly, or unknowingly, against you. This applies whether evil is coming from one person or from many people. Not only will it protect you, but it will also reflect back that evil to the sender. So the more they try to harm you, the more they will actually harm themselves!

Love

There is probably more interest in "love philtres" and "potions" than in any other form of magick. The vast majority of these, however, belong to the realm of fiction, wishful thinking, or pure psychology.

However, there are "spells", or rituals, that can be done which do seem, for whatever reason, to work. One of the best known, and seemingly most effective, is the one involving the use of "Poppets". The type of magick used is the *sympathetic* variety: the Poppets represent the lovers; whatever is done to the Poppets is, then, done to the lovers.

A Poppet is a specially prepared cloth doll representing a person. It is a simple rough figure cut from two pieces of cloth (*fig. 1*). Whilst cutting the cloth the operator should be thinking of—in fact *concentrating* on—the person the doll is to represent. It may then be worked on further, for example, by embroidering it with the facial features, special characteristics (e.g. beard and moustache on male; long hair on female), even astrological signs, etc., of the person, and sewn around leaving the top open (*fig. 2*). The figure is then stuffed with appropriate herbs, again while the actual person is being concentrated upon. The

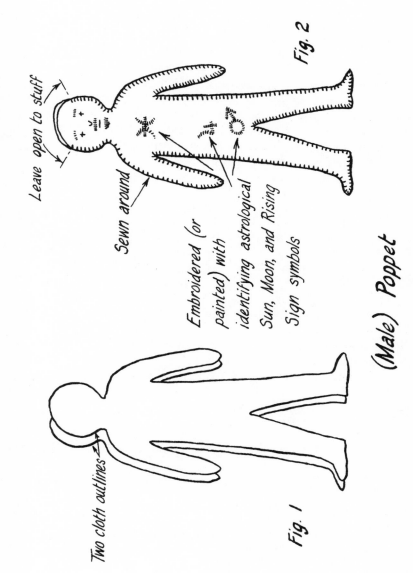

Two cloth outlines

Fig. 1

Leave open to stuff

Sewn around

Embroidered (or painted) with identifying astrological Sun, Moon, and Rising Sign symbols

Fig. 2

(Male) Poppet

97

herbs used for stuffing might be any of the following: Verbena, Vervain, Feverfew, Artemesia, Yarrow, Valerian, Motherwort, Rose buds, Elder, or Damiana. These are the herbs governed by Venus.

The top is then sewn up. Two figures are thus prepared; one representing the male, the other the female. If there is no definite "other lover" (i.e. if you are perhaps engaged in a search for the "ideal" mate) then the "other" figure should be made with all the characteristics being sought. In other words, if a man is seeking a girl with blue eyes and long blonde hair the female poppet should reflect this.

When the Poppets have been prepared, then the actual ritual can begin:

WARNING Since this ritual does seem to have effect it should not be used lightly. It is to bring about true, lasting, love; it should not be used to trigger a "passing affaire".

[This ritual should be performed within the Circle. It can be done with all the Coven present, or with just the Petitioner[2].] The *Erecting the Temple* is performed. Petitioner has prepared the Poppets and they lie on opposite sides of the Altar, in front of the Sword. Also on the Altar lies a length of ribbon. This is red in color and twenty-one inches in length.]

Petitioner: "O Mighty Woden and Loveliest Freya,
Hear now my plea to you.
My plea for true love
For . . . (Name) . . . and for . . . (Name)
. . ."
(*or* "For . . . (Name) . . . and for Another.")

[Petitioner takes up one of the Poppets and, dipping

---

[2] The "Petitioner" is the one "petitioning the gods". It might be one of the would-be lovers, or a third party acting on their behalf.

her fingers into the Salted Water, sprinkles it liberally all over. She then passes it through the smoke of the incense, turning it so that all parts get well censed. While doing this she says the following:]

Petitioner: "I name this Poppet . . . (Name) . . . ,
It is him/her in every way.
As he/she lives, so lives this Poppet.
Aught that I do to it
I do to him/her."

[Petitioner replaces the Poppet; picks up the other and sprinkles and censes it, saying:]

Petitioner: "I name this Poppet . . . (Name) . . . ,
(or "Man/Woman")
It is him/her in every way.
As he/she lives, so lives this Poppet.
Aught that I do to it
I do to him/her."

[Petitioner replaces Poppet, then kneels before the Altar with one hand resting lightly on each Poppet. With eyes closed Petitioner pictures, in her mind, the two represented people slowly coming together, meeting, kissing, and embracing. As she does this—which should not be hurried—she should slowly move the two Poppets, over the Sword, towards one another until eventually they meet. At this point she may open her eyes and, holding the Poppets together, face to face, say:]

Petitioner: "Thus may they be drawn
One to the other,
Strongly and truly.
To be together always
As One.
No more shall they be separated;
No more alone,
But ever fast together
As One."

[The Poppets should now be laid together, in the center of the Altar, with the Sword resting across on top of them. They should be allowed to remain there for ten minutes or more, whilst the Practitioner sits and meditates on the two people *together*—happy, laughing, enjoying one another's company, obviously "in love". Traditionally Friday is the day ruled by the Goddess of Love. This ritual should, then, be performed on a Friday. It should be repeated on the following two Fridays also—three consecutive Fridays in all. Between times, if they cannot be left on the Altar, the Poppets should be wrapped in a clean white cloth—still together—and put somewhere where they will not be disturbed.

On the final Friday, when the above ritual is performed, the Petitioner will conclude as follows:]

Petitioner: Now may Woden and Freya
Bind these two together,
As I do bind them here."

[Petitioner takes up the Poppets and binds the red ribbon several times around the two, tying the ends together about them.]

Petitioner: "Now are they forever one,
Even as the Gods themselves.
May each truly become a part of the other
That, separated, they would seem incomplete.
So be it!"

[Bound Poppets are placed beneath the Sword and, again, left for a few moments while Petitioner meditates. After completion of the ritual the Poppets should be wrapped in the clean white cloth and kept carefully where they will never be unbound.]

Healing

There are dozens, if not hundreds, of ways of working Magick. Many Witch Covens, of the different traditions, work much of their Magick for the healing of the sick. The different traditions have found their own favorite ways of working—those which seem most effective for them. Below is given a way of working Healing Magick as used in the Saxon tradition. It is, therefore, only one of many possible methods.

(N.B. Witches are not opposed to the medical profession! Far from it; if you are sick you should see a doctor, since he is specially trained to heal the sick. However, there are many instances where Magick can be used to supplement medical work or, in instances where a case might be considered "hopeless", where it can take up where the medical work left off.) The "central theme" of (Saxon) healing is mind-power. With a little training the mind is capable of summoning up a tremendous force from within the body and directing it to cause change.[3]

[3] Psychokinesis (PK) would be an example—movement of objects by thought alone, without physical contact. (See *Psychic Discoveries Behind the Iron Curtain*, Ostrander & Schroeder, N.Y., 1970)

[If there is healing to be done, in the Temple, then it should be done somewhere between the *Ceremony of Cakes and Ale* and the final *Clearing the Temple*. This "segment" of the Coven meeting is usually taken up with common discussion, conversation, relaxation, etc. At this time, then, there can be discussion of who is to be healed. The history of the person should be gone over and "approach" discussed (*see below*). All should be able to hold a clear picture of the Recipient in their mind. When all are ready the Coven rise and, holding hands, form a circle about the Altar.]

Priest: "Woden and Freya, be with us now."

Priestess: "Help us to draw the goodness from our bodies and send it where it is most needed."

Priest: "We ask your help, this time,
In sending our thought-force
To . . . (Name) . . .
Dire is his/her need;
Great is our will.
Let that which is ours
Be shared with him/her,
That all may be well."

[The Coven, holding hands, now start to move clockwise around the Altar. Starting slowly they gradually move faster and faster. This may be done as a walk-run, or as a dance with simple skip-step. Music may or may not be used[4]. The hands must not part throughout the Healing Rite. When the Priest or Priestess feels the Coven is sufficiently "worked up"[5] to produce the requisite energy, they will call a halt. The

---

[4] Some Covens have a musician or just a drummer beating out a rhythm. He sits off to one side. Of recorded music the opening few minutes of Carl Orff's *Carmina Burana* are ideal.

[5] A state of *ekstasis* (getting out of oneself) has been achieved.

Witches stop and stand (usually with eyes closed, to aid concentration) imagining—and feeling— the "energy" or "power" actually flowing out from their bodies. In their minds they form an image of the Recipient, the one to be healed[6], and see the energy flowing into him[7]. This is, again, continued until the Priest or Priestess feels the maximum available energy has been sent.]

Priestess: "We thank you, Woden and Freya both, for that which you have allowed us to achieve."

[The Coven then sits again, to rest[8], before the *Clearing the Temple.*]

---

[6] The "Approach" is the name of this image-forming, since it varies depending upon the particular need(s) of the Recipient. For example, should he be unable to walk then he is pictured walking, running, jumping, dancing, etc., completely fit and singing, laughing, shouting, etc. In other words, he is always pictured as *fully cured*—not *getting* better, but already well.

[7] Questioned on the appearance of the "energy/power" one Witch said it seemed like a bright, pure-white light which flowed out from her body and slowly enveloped the body of the sick person. Then it was as though that person's body gradually absorbed, or "soaked up", the light.

[8] As with many other forms of healing it is not uncommon for the healer(s) to feel thoroughly depleted, both physically and mentally, following a healing session.

Other Magick

There are occasions when it is felt that Magick may be of assistance other than for healing. However, the Witch considers Magick as "work". It should be done, therefore, only if there is a very real need for it. It is certainly never done "just to show that it can be done." The Witch knows it works and does not particularly care whether or not anyone else believes it!

The Saxons stress that two things should always be remembered, where Magick is concerned:

(i) Witchcraft is first and foremost a *religion*. Worship of the Gods is therefore the prime concern of the Witch. *Magick is secondary to that worship*. So no one should think of becoming a Witch just to learn to work Magick.

(ii) Magick must *never* be used to harm anyone.

Whatever the Magick is to be used for—be it to cause justice to be done in a court case (*Note*—it would not be used to make one particular person win, for they might, even unknowingly, be in the wrong; so it is done to "cause justice to be done"), or to help someone buy a house, or car, at a price she can afford—it would be worked in much the same way. The Priest and Priestess would state what was desired; the Coven would work up the energy to bring it about; the energy would be directed. This is the usual way of working Magick with the Seax-Wica. Other ways certainly could be tried by Covens.

Hwata (Divination)

Divination, or "augury", deals with attempting to find what the future holds. There are many different methods of trying to obtain this knowledge. Some of the best known are *cartomancy* (by cards), *cheiromancy* (by the palms of the hands), *tasseography* (by tea-leaves), and *scrying* (crystal- or mirror-gazing). Any form of divination is a practice in itself, and not a part of Witchcraft *per se*. In other words, although many Witches practice divination, so do many people who are not Witches. So just because your next-door-neighbor reads Tarot cards this does not make her a Witch!

There are many books on most forms of divination (*see Bibliography*) so here we shall look at only one or two *methods* which might be peculiar to the Seax-Wica.

The Saxon Wands[9]

Seven Wands are needed. These may be made from wood-dowelling. There should be three each nine inches in length, and four each twelve inches in length. One of the twelve-inch Wands should be marked, or decorated in some way, as the WITAN Wand.

Kneeling, lay the Witan Wand on the ground before you, horizontally "across" you. Take the other six wands and hold them out over the Witan Wand. Close your eyes and, holding them between your two hands, mix them together while concentrating on your question.

Keeping the eyes closed, grip the wands in your right hand; take the tip of one wand with the fingers of the left hand; concentrate for a moment longer on your question, then open your right hand. All the wands will fall to the ground except the one held now by your left hand. Open your eyes.

(1) If there are more LONG wands than short wands on

[9] This might—just possibly—have been inspired by the *I-Ching*, but it is certainly nowhere near as complicated as that ancient Chinese form of divination.

the ground then the answer to your question is in the Affirmative.

(2) If there are more SHORT wands than long wands on the ground (excluding the Witan Wand) then the answer is in the Negative.

(3) If any wand(s) touch the Witan Wand it means the answer will be a very definite one, with strong forces at work.

(4) If any wand(s) are off the ground (resting on others) circumstances are such (forces still working) that no definite answer can yet be given—regardless of (1) or (2).

(5) If *all* the wands point towards the Witan Wand then you (or the person for whom you are asking) will have a definite role to play in the determination of the question.

(6) If *none* of the wands point towards the Witan Wand then the matter will be determined without your (the Querent's) interference.

Tarot

There are many books on the Tarot, but the Seax-Wica feel that a true Reader should not just read interpretations from a book. A true Reader should go by what the particular card, in its especial position, means for the individual for whom she is reading at that time. In effect, then, the reading comes from *within* the Reader, or the Querent, or perhaps a combination of both. It then becomes a very *personal* interpretation of the symbols on the cards.

For an absolute beginner it is permissible to work with a book for a while. But as soon as possible the book should be dispensed with, and the Reader should go purely by "intuition". The decks most favored by the Seax-Wica are the Waite (Rider) deck; the Crowley "Thoth" deck; and the Grand Tarot Belline. Of the layouts used many favor the Celtic Cross. There is, however, one which seems little known outside the Seax-Wica. They call it "The Path" layout:

The Path

The Reader goes through the complete deck (all 78 cards) to find the Significator—the card to represent the Querent. This Significator is chosen by the "feel", the "vibes", that the Reader gets to tell her that this is *the one special card* that represents the Querent. The rest of the deck (77 cards) is then handed to the Querent, who shuffles them and generally handles them while concentrating on any particular question he wishes to ask. After a few moments of such shuffling the Querent lays the deck *face down*, spread out across the table in front of him. He selects eight cards, at random, keeping them face down. These are the only ones used for the reading.

The Reader lays out the cards, still face down, to the following pattern, ready for the interpretation:

The Path

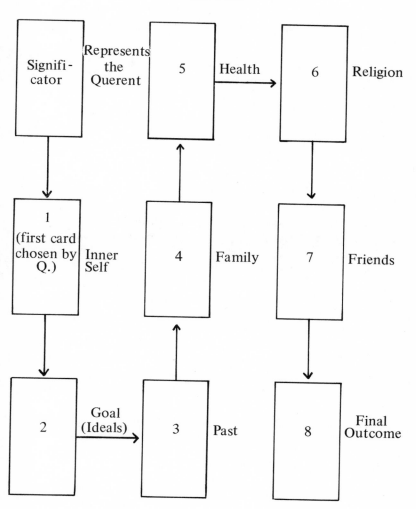

Turning the cards over, one at a time, the Reader interprets the symbolism of each card, according to the meaning of its position (Health, Religion, etc.).

Scrying

The two most common forms of scrying are Crystal-Gazing and Mirror-Gazing. Both are done in much the same way.

Crystal-Gazing

The crystal should be without flaw—no scratches on the surface, nor bubbles within. (The new acrylic-plexiglass "crystals" work quite well, but scratch extremely easily. Care is therefore needed in handling them).

Rest the ball on a background of black. A black velvet cloth is ideal. This can, in turn, rest on a table in front of you or can cover your hand(s) as you hold the crystal. This black background is to ensure that you see nothing around the ball to distract you, as you gaze into it.

Initially you should work alone, in a room that is quiet and dark. Have just one small light—perhaps a candle. Place the light so that you do not see it reflected directly in the crystal. Burn a pleasant-smelling incense, as it will help you concentrate. Then sit and gaze into the crystal *trying to keep your mind blank*. This is not easy and will take some practice.

Do not *stare* at the ball, unblinking. This will only cause eyestrain! Gaze—blinking the eyes naturally, as necessary. Do not try to imagine anything *in* the ball. Just try to keep the mind blank. After a while it will seem that the ball is filling with white mist, or smoke. It will gradually grow more and more dense until the ball seems full of it. Then, again gradually, the smoke will thin and fade, leaving behind a picture—almost like a miniature television set! It might be in black-and-white but is more likely to be in color. It might be still or it might be moving. It might be from the past, the present, or the future. Also it might well be a symbolic picture, requiring some interpretation.

Initially you have no great control over what you see. You must just take what comes. As you become more adept you may meditate for a few moments, *before* gazing, on what you wish to see. Then, when you start to gaze, clear your mind and try to keep it blank.

Most people seem capable of success at scrying. If you get nothing the first time you try, then try the next night, and the next. Do not try for more than ten minutes or so at each attempt, however.

Mirror-Gazing

A black mirror is generally the best for mirror-gazing. You can make one according to the lengthy, involved instructions to be found in some of the Ceremonial Magick *grimoires*, or you can take a regular piece of glass [10] and spray the back of it with a good black enamel. Either works as well as the other.

The *modus operandi* is the same as with the crystal, above, though the image appears, gradually, without the introductory white smoke.

---

[10] It is especially effective if you can find an oval, *concave*, piece of glass.

Another form of Scrying frequently employed by the Seax-Wica is:

Fire-Fantasy

Make a fire[11] of driftwood, on the sea-shore, after sunset.[12] When the wood has been well-burned and is beginning to die down, lay on it a cedar log, a juniper log, and three good handfuls of sandalwood chips. Let these burn well. Then, as the fire again begins to die down, gaze deep into the dying embers. In these embers you will see scenes of the past, the present, and the future. You may see the actual scenes. But it is more likely that you will see symbolic scenes—frequently with mythical beasts and birds.

[11] Sometimes called "The Fire of Azrael".

[12] If far from the sea, use old, weathered wood.

Lacnunga (Herbal Lore)

Individual Gesiths may keep their own "TREE" if they so wish. In it they might well keep notes on items of special personal interest, such as astrology, tarot, herbal lore, etc. What follows below were the notes, in an old book, concerning Herbs—their preparation and use. This would probably be used in conjunction with one of the old herbals, such as Gerard's or Culpeper's.

The Gathering, Drying, and Keeping of Simples and their juices

1. Leaves of herbs, or of trees.

Choose only the leaves that are green and full of juice. Pick them carefully and throw away any that are bruised or damaged, for they would spoil the rest. Note where they grow best and gather them there. For example, betony growing in the shade is better than betony growing in the sun, since it seems to prefer the shade. Similarly some herbs prefer to grow near water so, although you may find some growing away from water, gather only those that are near water. The leaves of such herbs that seed are better before they flower than after.

Dry the leaves well in the sun, then lay them between sheets of brown paper or, better still, in brown paper bags. Press them a little and store them in a dry place—if possible, near the fire. It is not possible to give a general drying time for all leaves; those that grow on dry grounds will keep better than those that grow on moist grounds. Herbs that are full of juice will not keep so long as those that are naturally drier. Herbs that are well dried will keep longer than those that are slack dried. You can tell when they have lost their virtues by the loss of color and/or smell.

2. *Flowers.*

The flower should be gathered when in its prime. As for the time of day, it should be when the sun shines upon them, so that they are dry—for if you gather flowers or herbs when they are wet they will not keep.

Dry flowers as you do leaves: between brown paper, near a fire. Again, when they lose their color/smell then have they lost their virtue.

3. *Seeds.*

The seed is that part of the plant which can bring forth its like. They should be gathered from the places where they best prefer to grow. The seeds should be fully ripe when gathered, should be dried just a little in the sun before storing them in brown paper. There is not the necessity to store them near the fire. They are best within the first year after they are gathered, but will actually keep for years.

4. *Roots.*

Discard any roots that are worm-eaten or rotten. Use only those that have good color, taste, and smell. They should be neither too soft nor too hard. The drier roots are, when you gather them, the better, for they have the less moisture in them. Such roots as are hard can be dried where you will; those that are soft are best dried in the sun or hung, by a string, near the fire. Larger roots will keep longer than smaller ones. Most will keep for roughly a year.

With soft roots it is best to always keep them near the fire. Sometimes, in the winter time, you will find that the herbs, roots, flowers are moist. They should be dried by a gentle fire, and if possible always kept near it. It is pointless to dry roots that are always plentiful. Far better to just gather them when you need them.

5. *Barks.*

Barks are of fruits, roots, and boughs. The barks of fruits (e.g. oranges, lemons, etc.) are best taken when the fruit is fully ripe. The barks of trees are best gathered in the Spring, for then they come off more easily and you can dry them as you please.

For the "barks" of roots taken from such herbs as have pith in them (e.g. parsley, fennel, etc.), they should be slit up the middle and the pith removed. The remains is called, improperly, the "bark", and is to be used.

6. *Juices.*

Juices should be pressed out of herbs when they are young and tender. They can be pressed out of some stalks and tender tops of herbs and plants, and also out of some flowers. If you have gathered the herb and it is dry, bruise it well in a stone[13] mortar with a wooden pestle. Then place the herb in a canvas bag and press it hard in a press. Collect the juice and clarify it.

To clarify the juice: put it into a pipkin[14] or skillet, or something similar, and stand it over a fire. Let it stand there till all the scum rises to the top. Scoop off the scum and discard it. You are now left with the clarified juice. There are two ways to prepare this to keep for up to a year:

(i) When cold pour the juice into a glass and cover it with about two inches of oil. The oil will stay on top, keeping the air from putrifying it. When you intend to use the juice pour it off into a porringer[15]. If any oil comes out with it just scoop it off with a spoon. Unused juice may be poured back in the glass, since it will then sink down through the oil.

---

[13] Not a wooden one, which would tend to absorb the juice.

[14] A small earthen boiler.

[15] A small bowl used for porridge, cereal, etc.

(ii) When clarified boil the juice over the fire till, when left to get cold, it becomes of the thickness of honey. This is most commonly used for diseases of the mouth.

The Way of Making and Keeping all Necessary Compounds

Above has been discussed Simples—medicines in their natural form. Now here are ways to treat artificial medicines.

1. *Syrups.*
A syrup is a medicine in liquid form, composed of infusion, decoction, and juice.

(a) INFUSION—Syrups made by infusion are usually made of flowers. The flowers used are those, like roses and violets, that soon lose their color and strength by boiling. Having picked your flowers, to each pound add three pints of spring water. Bring the water to a boil, then pour it over the flowers as they lie in a pewter pot. Cover the pot and let it stand by the fire, keeping hot, for twelve hours. Then strain off the liquid into a pewter or glazed-earthenware basin. (To make a stronger infusion, then repeat the above adding fresh flowers to the liquid in the same proportions.) To every pint of the liquid add two pounds of sugar. Being only melted over the fire, without being boiled, this will give you the syrup you desire.

(b) DECOCTION—Syrups made of decoctions are

usually made of compounds, yet any simple herb can be converted into syrup. First slightly bruise the herb, root, or flower, then boil it in a convenient quantity of spring water (the more water you boil it in the weaker it will be). A handful of the root to a pint of water is a good proportion. Boil it till half the water is consumed then let it stand till it is almost cold. Strain it, then, through a woollen cloth, but allow it to strain itself, rather than pressing it through. To every pint of this decoction add one pound of sugar and boil it till it comes to a syrup (you can judge this by now and then cooling a little in a spoon). Skim it all the while it boils then, when it is sufficiently boiled and while it is still hot, strain it again through a piece of woollen cloth. Then you have the syrup.

(c) JUICE—Using such herbs as are full of juice, beat the herb in a stone mortar with a wooden pestle. Press out the juice and clarify it (see above). Then let the juice boil away until about a quarter of it has been consumed. To a pint of the remaining then add a pound of sugar and boil it to a syrup, always skimming it. When it is sufficiently boiled strain it through a woollen cloth, as above. If you make a syrup of roots, when you have bruised them let them steep in the water you are going to use to boil them. Have the water hot.

Keep your syrups in glasses or stone pots but seal them with waxed paper tied over the mouth. If corked they can explode. Most syrups will keep for at least a year. Those made by infusion keep a shorter time than the others.

2. *Juleps*.

A julep is nothing more than a pleasant potion. It is often used (i) to prepare the body for purgation, (ii) to open obstructions, and the pores, (iii) to digest tough humors, (iv) to qualify hot distempers, etc.

Take a pint of distilled water to which add two ounces of syrup (see 3 below); mix them and drink when you feel the need. If you prefer a tart taste add ten drops of vitrol to the pint and shake well.

All juleps are made for immediate use and should not, therefore, be stored.

3. *Decoctions.*

The difference between decoctions and syrups made by decoction is that syrups are made to keep, while decoctions are for immediate use (actually they may be kept for up to one week at the most). Decoctions are made of leaves, roots, flowers, seeds, fruits, or barks, and are made in the manner described above under "SYRUPS".

Decoctions made with wine last longer than those made with water. If you are using a decoction to cleanse the passage of urine, or open obstructions, then make it with *white* wine rather than water, since this is more penetrating. Decoctions are most useful in diseases concerning the passage of the body, i.e. stomach, bowels, kidneys, urinal passage, bladder, etc. If you wish to sweeten a decoction, either with sugar or with syrup, you may do so without unduly affecting it.

If, in a decoction, you boil roots, herbs, flowers, and seeds together then let the roots boil for a good time longer than the others. Next in order would be the barks, then herbs, seeds, flowers. If you should mix in spices these should be boiled for the shortest time. When boiling such as figs, quince-seed, linseed—the types that cause a sliminess through boiling—tie them first in a piece of linen, before boiling.

All decoctions should be kept in a glass jar, firmly stopped, and kept in a cool place.

The usual dosage, at one time is from two to five ounces, according to the age and strength of the invalid.

4. *Oils.*

Olive oil is the finest oil, being pressed from ripe olives. Some oils are simple; some are compound.

124

Simple oils are those made from fuits or seeds, by pressing, such as oil of almonds, linseed, etc. Compound oils are those made from olive oil mixed with other simples such as herbs, flowers, roots, etc.

Having bruised the herbs or flowers put them into an earthen pot. To two or three handfuls of them add a pint of oil. Cover the pot with paper and let it stand out in the sun for approximately two weeks (depending upon the amount of sunshine). Then, after warming it well before a fire, press out the herb in a press and add the same number of herbs again to that oil—bruising them first. Repeat the process of standing them out in the sun, etc. Continue until the oil is as strong as you wish—the more times you bruise herbs and add them, the stronger will the oil become. Finally, when strong enough, boil both oil and herbs together till the juice is consumed (this you will know because the bubbling will cease and the herbs will become crisp). Then strain it, while it is hot, and keep it in a stone or glass vessel.

The usual use of these oils is for pains in the limbs, roughness of the skin, itching, etc. If you wish to use oil on wounds then first dissolve an ounce of turpentine to each two ounces of oil (mixing over heat) so that the oil does not aggravate the wound.

5. *Electuaries*

It is as well to be prepared for the making of electuaries by keeping dried herbs, roots, flowers, seeds, etc., on hand. Take the required herb and beat it into a powder (if it is not dry enough then dry it slowly by a fire). Sieve the powder so that you get only the finest. To one ounce of the powder add three ounces of clarified honey, and mix them well together. (*Note:* to clarify honey, set it over a fire till the scum rises. Scoop this off and leave the clarified honey.)

The usual dosage of cordial electuaries is from half a dram to two drams; of purging electuaries, from half an ounce to an ounce. They should be taken either on rising or just before retiring.

6. *Conserves.*

There are two ways of making conserves: one with herbs and flowers, the other with fruit.

Using herbs and flowers (such as wormwood, rue, scurvy grass, etc.): take only the leaves and the tender tops and, having beaten them, weigh them. Be sure to beat them well. Then, to each pound add three pounds of sugar.

Using fruit (such as sloes, barberries, etc.): first scald the fruit, then rub the pulp through a thick sieve (a pulping sieve). Add to it an equal amount/weight of sugar and place in a pewter vessel over a charcoal fire. Stir till the sugar is melted, resulting in conserve.

Dosage of conserves is usually an amount the size of a nutmeg, given morning and evening. Conserves should be kept in an earthen pot. They may keep for only a year—as with conserve of borage, cowslips, bugloss—or for many years—as with conserve of roses. Should you find the conserve has developed a hard crust on the top, sometimes perforated with what look like small worm-holes, then you know the conserve is almost spoiled and has lost its efficacy.

7. *Preserves.*

Preserves are made with sugar. There are four main types: (i) Flowers (ii) Fruits (iii) Roots (iv) Barks.

(i) Flowers—These are seldom preserved, but can be done this way. Take a large jar and cover the bottom with a layer of fine sugar. On that strew a layer of flowers. Cover with another layer of fine sugar, one of flowers, of sugar, and so on till the jar is filled. Then tie paper over the top of the jar and leave for a short time.

(ii) Fruits—There are two methods of preserving fruits: (a) Boil them well in water, then pulp them through a sieve. With an equal amount of sugar (i.e. one pound sugar to one pint water) boil the water they were boiled in into a syrup. To every pound of this syrup add four ounces of the pulp. Boil this over a gentle fire, to the right consistency—if you drop a spot of the syrup onto a trencher, when cold it will not stick to your fingers. (b) Another way to preserve fruit is to first pare off the rind, then cut the fruit in halves and remove the core. Then boil in water till soft, and remove. Then boil that same water, with an equal amount of sugar, into a syrup. Put the syrup into a pot and add the boiled fruit. Let it remain there till you need it.

(iii) Roots—First scrape clean and cleanse of the pith, if they have any. Boil in water till soft, then remove them. Add an equal amount of sugar to the water and boil to a syrup. Place the roots in that syrup, in a pot, and keep till needed.

(iv) Barks (meaning oranges, lemons, citrons, etc.)—First boil the barks whole till soft. Make a syrup of the water and keep them in the syrup—as with roots, above.

Preserves may be kept in glass jars or in glazed pots. Flowers will keep a year; roots and barks much longer.

8.*Ointments.*

Bruise the herb, flower, or root to be used, and to two handfuls add one pound of hog's grease dried, or cleansed from the skins. Beat them well together with a wooden pestle in a stone mortar, then put into a stone pot and cover with paper. Place it in the sun, or in some warm place, for three to five days. Next take the mixture and boil it a little, then when hot strain it out, pressing it hard in a press. To this grease add as many more herbs as before and repeat the above. This may be repeated two or three times more. Finally, to every pound of ointment add two ounces of turpentine and two ounces of wax. Kept in a pot ointments will last over two years.

9. *Poultices.*

Poultices are made of herbs and roots chopped small

and boiled in water to a jelly. Add a little barley meal, or meal of lupins, and a little oil or rough sweet suet. Spread over a cloth and apply to the wound.

Poultices will ease pains, break sores, cool inflamations, dissolve hardness, dissipate swellings, etc.

It should again be mentioned that to find which herbs, flowers, etc. should be used for which ailments the above would be used in conjunction with some such herbal as Culpeper's or Gerard's.

Appendix 'A' — Magickal Alphabets

In the early Middle Ages many practitioners of Ceremonial Magick utilized secret alphabets to protect their works from prying eyes. Many of these alphabets are known today and are still used, not only by Magicians but also by Witches and other occult practitioners. A few of the better known alphabets are given below.

Theban
The "official" magickal alphabet of Gardnerian, and other, Witches. It has been called, incorrectly, "The Witches' Runes" and "The Witches' Alphabet". It originated with the Ceremonial Magicians and was only adopted by some Craft traditions in recent times.

Passing the River
This was used almost exclusively by the Ceremonial Magicians. Its only appearance in Witchcraft today might be on certain talismans (good luck charms), depending on the individual Witch making it.

Angelic, or Celestial
As with "Passing the River".

Language of the Magi, or Malachim

A	૧	O	ၮ
B	૧	P	ၮ
C	ᄳ	Q	ၣ
D	ၮ	R	ၮ
E	ひ	S	४
F	ᄴ	T	ၮ
G	ၯ	U,V	ၣ
H	४	X	ၮ
I,J	ซ	Y	ၮ
K	ᄱ	Z	ၮ
L	ช		
M	ठ		
N	ၮ		

Symbol designating
the end of a sentence   ᄯᄭᄽ

The Theban Alphabet

① Passing the River ② Malachim ③ Celestial

Magickal Alphabets

As with "Passing the River".

Egyptian Heiroglyphs
Frequently used in some of the esoteric magickal orders. Particularly, of course, those with a pseudo-Egyptian background. Seldom, if ever, found in Witchcraft.
(See *Egyptian Language*, Sir Wallis Budge, Dover, New York)

Ogam Bethluisnion
The writing of the early Celts and of their priests, the Druids. An extremely simple form of writing, especially useful for carving inscriptions along the edge of a stone or piece of wood.

Runes
The word *Rune* means "mystery" or "secret" in early English and related languages. It is certainly heavily charged with overtones, and for good reason. Runes were never a strictly utilitarian script. From their earliest adaption into Germanic usage they served for divinitory and ritual uses.
There are to be found more variations of Runes than of any other alphabet, it seems. Adopted by Witches and Magicians alike, Runic served as a very popular form of occult writing. There are three main types of Runes: Germanic, Scandinavian, and Anglo-Saxon. They each, in turn, have any number of sub-divisions/variations.
Looking first at the GERMANIC, there are basically twenty-four different runes employed, though variations may be found in different areas. A common name for the Germanic Runes is *futhark*, after the first six letters ("th" is one letter—Þ). In the SCANDINAVIAN (Danish and Swedish-Norwegian, or Norse) are found sixteen runes, again with (innumerable) variations.
The ANGLO-SAXON Runes vary in number, anywhere from twenty-eight to thirty-one. In fact by

Ogam Bethluisnion

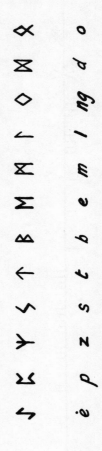

Germanic Runes

134

the ninth century, in Northumbria, we find thirty-three runes. A common name for the Anglo-Saxon Runes is *futhorc*, again from the first six letters.

A "Celtic" form of Runes is sometimes employed by Gardnerian and Celtic Covens.

The "Saxon" Runes, as detailed on page 17, are the ones favored by the Seax-Wica.

DANISH

ᛒ ᚼ ᚠ ᚱ ᚴ ᚼ ᛬ ᛁ ᛐ ᛌ ᛏ ᛒ ᛘ ᛚ ᛦ

f u th a r k h n i a s t b m l R

SWEDISH - NORSE

ᚠ ᚼ ᚠ ᚱ ᚴ ᛏ ᚼ ᛁ ᛁ ᛌ ᛏ ᛒ ᛘ ᛚ ᛦ

f u th a r k h n i a s t b m l R

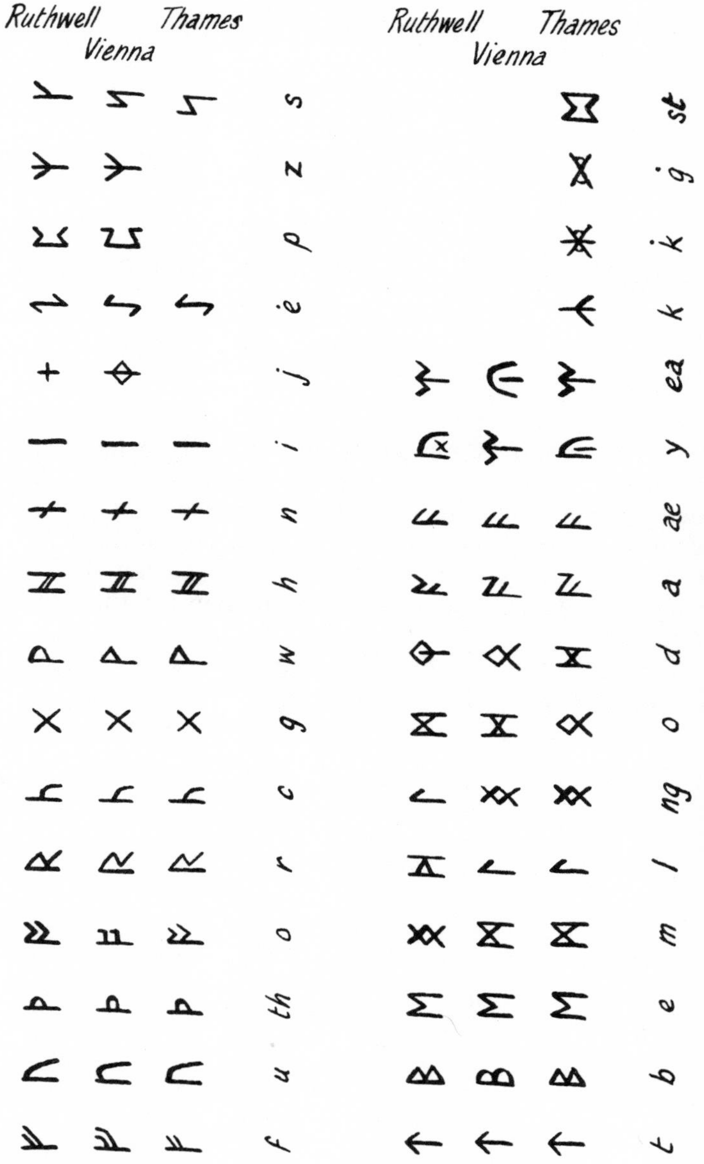

Ruthwell	Vienna	Thames	
�			s
⅄	⅄		z
⊠	⊠		p
⇃	⤳	⤳	ë
+	◈		j
—	—	—	i
✝	✝	✝	n
⅂	⅂	⅂	h
◁	◁	◁	w
✕	✕	✕	g
⌐	⌐	⌐	c
⋉	⋈	⋈	r
⩊	⫪	⩊	o
◿	◿	◿	th
⊂	⊂	⊂	u
⍯	⍯	⍯	f

Ruthwell	Vienna	Thames	
		⊠	st
		✕	g
		✳	k
		⟨	k
⅄	⊂	⅄	ea
⟨x⟩	⅄	⊏	y
⫫	⫫	⫫	ae
⟋	⟋	⟋	a
◈	◇	✕	d
⊠	⊠	◇	o
⌐	✕	✕	ng
⊼	⌐	⌐	l
✕	⊠	⊠	m
Ɱ	Ɱ	Ɱ	e
◿	B	◿	b
←	←	←	t

Anglo-Saxon Runes

137

Appendix 'B' — Seax-Wican Songs

In the old days there was much festivity at the Sabbat meetings. There were songs and dancing, games and frivolity. So it should be today. Victor Anderson has recently published an original collection of Pagan songs (*Thorns of the Blood Rose*, Anderson, California, 1970) written by himself. Some Covens have gathered older songs and dances, or made up their own for their own use.

Here are some of the old songs and dances used by various Covens of the Seax-Wica.

"THE MAYPOLE"

Come, ye young men, come a-long, With your mu-sic, dance and song;

Bring your las-ses in your hands, For 'tis that which love com-mands.

Then to the May-pole come a- way, For it is now a hol- i- day.

Repeat in Chorus

It is the choice time of the year,
For the violets now appear;
Now the rose receives its birth,
And pretty primrose decks the earth.
Then to the Maypole come away,
For it is now a holiday.

139

Here each bachelor may choose
One that will not faith abuse;
Now repay with coy disdain
Love that should be lov'd again.
    Then to the Maypole come away,
    For it is now a holiday.

And when you well reckoned have,
What kisses you your sweethearts gave,
Take them all again, and more,
It will never make them poor.
    Then to the Maypole come away,
    For it is now a holiday.

When you thus have spent the time,
Till the day be past its prime,
To your beds repair at night,
And dream there of your day's delight.
    Then to the Maypole haste away,
    For it is a holiday.

140

"AT A MAYPOLE DOWN IN KENT"

At a May-pole down in Kent, Now Spring with flow'-ry sweets has come,

Nymphs with swains to danc-ing went, Each hop'd to bear the gar-land home. When

Fre-ya came they all gave way; Youths with joy their hom-age pay,

Nymphs con-fess her Queen of May, No one was ev-er yet so gay.

All around your steps advance,
Now foot it in a fairy ring,
Nimbly trip and nimbly dance,
"Ever live bright Freya" sing.
With boughs their hearts of oak beset
Your brave sires their conqueror met,
No crown but her locks of jet
Now does your free allegiance get.

"FILL, FILL THE BRIGHT MEAD-CUP"

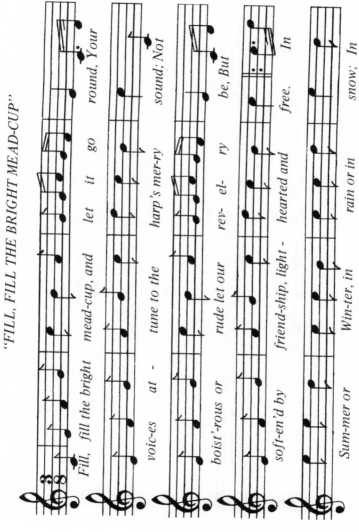

Fill, fill the bright mead-cup, and let it go round, Your
voic-es at - tune to the harp's mer-ry sound; Not
boist'-rous or rude let our rev- el- ry be, But
soft-en'd by friend-ship, light - hearted and free. In
Sum-mer or Win-ter, in rain or in snow; In

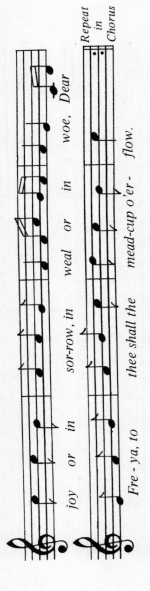

Amid the dear scenes of our Seax-Wica youth,
May virtue long flourish with freedom and truth;
And as we revisit each time-hallowed spot,
"The joy of the mead-cup" shall ne'er be forgot!
In Summer or Winter, in rain or in snow;
In joy or in sorrow, in weal or in woe,
Dear Freya, to thee shall the mead-cup o'erflow.

"THE FAIRY QUEEN"

Come, follow, follow me, Ye fairy elves that be, Come
follow Mab your queen, And trip it o'er the green,
Hand in hand we'll dance a-round, Be- cause this place is fairy ground.

Then o'er the mushroom's head
Our tablecloth we spread;
A grain of rye or wheat,
The diet that we eat;
Pearly drops of dew we drink
In acorn cups fill'd to the brink.

145

O'er tops of dewy grass
So nimbly do we pass,
The young and tender stalk
Ne'er bends where we do walk:
Yet in the morning may be seen
Where we the night before have been.

The folklore of Witches and Fairies often overlapped. See The Witch Cult in Western Europe, (Appendix I), Margaret Murray, Oxford Paperbacks, 1962. Witchcraft Today, (Ch. V), Gerald Gardner, Rider, 1954. Witchcraft From the Inside, (Ch. X), Raymond Buckland, Llewellyn, 1971.

"SEND ROUND THE CUP"

Send round the cup,   Fill, fill it up   To the friend we love so well.

Singing, piping, dancing,Or on charger prancing,Black Sir Harry bears the bell.

Soon as morn ap-pear-ing Tips the hills with gold, Hear him onward cheering, Steed and hun-ter bold:

While they fly ca-reer-ing, O-ver hill and dell, Black Sir Har-ry bears the bell.

Sing after me,
With merry glee,
To the world his praises tell:
Laughing, joking, sporting,
Pretty maidens courting,
Over all he hears the bell.
Who is like Sir Harry
In the banquet hall,
Chanting "Hey, down, derry,"
Giving joy to all?
Pledge in mead and perry,
Bumpers to our host;
"Black Sir Harry!" be the toast.

148

Appendix 'C' –
Seax-Wica Recipes
for Wine, Beer, and Ale

Home-made wine-making is a comparatively simple process. It is enjoying considerable vogue at present with various wine-making "kits" on the market. The Seax-Wica, however, prefer to make their own with the *real* ingredients—rather than using "Packet number one", "Packet number two", "Coloring", "flavoring", etc.

Cowslip Wine
Boil two pounds of white sugar with five quarts of water, and pour whilst boiling over a quart of the yellow part of fresh cowslip flowers. Leave for twenty-four hours, then strain and add two tablespoonfuls of yeast spread on a piece of toast. Leave, covered, for ten days, stirring two or three times each day for the first four. Then strain and bottle.

Dandelion Wine
The flowers must be freshly picked and the petals stripped from them. Put a gallon of these petals into a tub, and pour a gallon of freshly-boiled water over them. Leave, covered, for ten to twelve days, stirring now and then, and then strain the liquid into a preserving-pan and add three to four pounds of sugar according to your taste. Add also the thinly-pared rind

of an orange and a lemon and the rest of these two fruits cut in pieces without any trace of white pith or pits. Boil gently together for twenty minutes, and after it has cooled to luke-warm put in a tablespoonful of brewers' yeast or a quarter of an ounce of compressed yeast spread on a piece of toast. Cover again, and leave for a couple of days, then put it into a cask, bung it down, and bottle after two months or longer.

Potato Wine

Peel and slice enough potatoes to make a pound of slices, and put them into a pan with four pints of water. Cook until tender, then strain off the liquid and add for each quart half a pound of sugar, two ounces of raisins, two ounces of pearl barley, and a quarter of an ounce of yeast when it is luke-warm. Let it ferment, then filter into a cask or jar after it has settled for three days. Add isinglass at the rate of a quarter of an ounce to the gallon, cork tightly and leave to mature.

Rice Wine

Put three pounds of rice into a bowl with three pounds of sugar and a pound of raisins, add four quarts of water and then an ounce of yeast dissolved in a little warm water. Stand in the warm for twelve days, stirring now and then, skim, strain and pour into a stone jar. Cork securely and keep in the cool for six months before bottling.

Tomato Wine

Take the stalks off some sound, ripe, tomatoes, and cut them in pieces with a stainless steel knife. Then mash them well, and let them drain through a hair-sieve. Season the juice with a little salt and sugar to taste, then nearly fill a jar with it. Cover fairly closely, leaving a small hole for the fermentation to work through, and leave until this process has ended. Pour off the clear liquid into bottles, cork them tightly, and keep for some time before using it.

Bee Wine

Into a syrup solution of two tablespoonfuls of sugar to a pint of water put a very small pinch of tartaric acid and a piece of yeast the size of a dime. Start it off at blood heat and stand the glass jar in a warm room near the window, and leave it to work. In a day or so the yeast will begin to grow and collect bubbles so that the lump floats up and down. Fermentation will proceed until the liquid is converted into a sweet wine, which you may flavor if you wish by adding fruit juice. Do not let it work too long or it will become sour and eventually turn to vinegar.

Apple Beer

Pour four gallons of boiling water over four pounds of grated apples in a pan, and stir each day for two weeks. Then strain and add two pounds of sugar, two ounces of root ginger and a level teaspoonful each of cinnamon stick and whole cloves. Pour into a cask and bung tightly at once, and in six weeks it will be ready to bottle.

Honey Beer

Boil an ounce of ground ginger with half a gallon of water for half an hour, then put it into a pan with a pound of white sugar, two ounces of lime juice, four ounces of clean-run honey, the juice of three lemons, and another half gallon of cold water. When the mixture is just luke-warm, add a large teaspoonful of yeast spread on a piece of toast. Leave for twelve hours, and then strain through muslin. After giving it an hour or two to settle, bottle it carefully.

Cowslip Ale

Boil a gallon of water with two pounds of honey for three-quarters of an hour, uncovered, skimming it well.

Then take a pint of this and pour it over a large sliced lemon in a separate bowl. Pour the rest of the syrup over a gallon of cowslip flowers in another bowl, stir well, cover and leave in a warm place for twenty-four hours. Now stir in the lemon-flavored syrup, add two sprigs of sweet briar if you can, though this is not essential, and a quarter of an ounce of yeast dissolved in a little honey. Let this work for four days, strain into a cask, and keep in a cool place for six months before bottling.

Mead

Dissolve four pounds of honey in a gallon of water, and add an ounce of hops, half an ounce of root ginger, and the pared rind of two lemons. Boil this for three-quarters of an hour, pour it into a cask to the brim, and when it is still lukewarm add an ounce of yeast. Leave the mead to ferment, and when this has ended, put in a quarter of an ounce of isinglass and bung the cask tightly. In six months it should be bottled.

Appendix 'D' – Paganism

Just as the word "Christian" is a general term covering many different denominations (e.g. Roman Catholics, Baptists, Methodists, etc.) so is "Pagan" a general term covering the different traditions of Witchcraft together with many other non-Christian teachings. "Pagan" itself comes from the Latin *pagani*, meaning "one who dwells in the country". In the early days of Christianity the New Religion was found in the cities and the towns before it spread out to the villages and the country people. In those days, then, to speak of the *pagani* was to speak of those who were probably still following the Old Religion; the old, non-Christian, ways. "Pagan" gradually became, then, a term applied to any non-Christian (*Heathen*—one who lives on the heath—is applied in the same way, for the same reasons).

From the above it can be seen that all Witches would be termed Pagans (as would, for example, all Baptists be termed Christians), yet not all Pagans could be termed Witches (nor all Christians termed Baptists). I have risked belaboring the point because there are many Pagan groups in this country who, although worshipping the Gods of Nature in some form, would certainly object to being referred to as Witches. There are also many people who would be interested in joining a group of (generalized) Pagan persuasion without, at least initially, committing themselves to a particular tradition of Witchcraft. For such people an organization was formed called *The Pagan Way*. It puts out material on many aspects of Paganism and helps the formation of worship groups. Many people use the Pagan Way as a stepping-stone to Witchcraft specifically; a gradual "easing-in" to the Old Religion. There are several distribution points throughout the country for their material:

New York and Long Island —
Ed. Buczynski, 300 Henry Street, Brooklyn, N.Y. 11201

Northern New Jersey —
Pagan Way, Box 596, Passaic, N.J. 07055

Chicago Metropolitan Area —
Pagan Way, 1125 W. Wellington Avenue, Chicago, Ill. 60657

Louisville, Kentucky —
Covenstead Museum, 128 W. College St., Louisville, Ky. 40202

South Dakota —
Pagan Way, Box 593, Huron, South Dakota 57350

Los Angeles Area —
Pagan Way, Box 723, Pasadena, California 91102

Today there are a number of publications available to those interested in just about any aspect of Paganism. Some of the better ones are listed hereunder:

CRYSTAL WELL, THE (formerly "The Waxing Moon"), Box 18351, Philadelphia, Pa. 19120

EARTH RELIGION NEWS, 300 Henry Street, Brooklyn, New York, 11201

GNOSTICA NEWS, Box 3383, St. Paul, Minnesota 55165

GREEN EGG, THE, Box 2953, St. Louis, Missouri 63130

KORYTHALIA, Box 691, Altadena, California 91001

NEMETON, Box 13037, Oakland, California 94661

NEW BROOM, THE, Box 1646, Dallas, Texas 74221

PAGAN, THE, Box 2953, St. Louis, Missouri 63130

RUNESTONE, THE, Box 2442, Wichita Falls, Texas 76301

SEAX-WICA, Buckland, Box 238, Weirs Beach, New Hampshire 03246

SILVER ANKH, THE, 565 Howard Drive NE, Sierra Vista, Arizona 85635

WICA NEWSLETTER, Hero Press, Suite 1B, 153 West 80th Street, New York, N.Y. 10024

WITCHES' TRINE, THE, 3125 Harrison Street, Oakland, Calif. 94611

X, Rod Frye, Box 7374, Hampton, Virginia 23366

Bibliography

Anderson, V.   *Thorns of the Blood Rose*, Anderson, California, 1970.

Bracelin, J.   *Gerald Gardner: Witch*, Octagon Press, London, nd.

Branston, B.   *The Lost Gods of England*, Thames and Hudson, London, 1957.

Buckland, R.   *A Pocket Guide to the Supernatural*, Ace Books, New York, 1969.
                  Witchcraft Ancient and Modern, H.C. Publishers, New York, 1970.
                  Witchcraft From the Inside, Llewellyn, Minn., 1971.

Crowther, P. & A. *The Witches Speak*, Athol, Isle of Man, 1965.

Culpeper, N.   *Culpeper's Complete Herbal*, Foulsham, London, nd.

Eliade, M.   *Rites and Symbols of Initiation*, Harper, N.Y., 1958.

156

Frazer, Sir J.   *The Golden Bough*, Macmillan, New York, 1922.

Gardner, G.   *Witchcraft Today*, Citadel, New York, 1970.
The Meaning of Witchcraft, Weiser, N.Y., 1972.

Gibbons, E.   *Stalking the Healthful Herbs*, McKay, N.Y., 1966.

Glass, J.   *Witchcraft, the Sixth Sense*, Wilshire, No. Hollywood, 1973.

Graves, R.   *The White Goddess*, Noonday Press, N.Y., 1966.

Gray, E.   *The Tarot Revealed*, Inspiration House, N.Y., 1960.

Leland, C.   *Aradia, Gospel of the Witches*, Buckland Museum, New York, 1969.

Lethbridge, T.   *Witches*, Routledge & Kegan Paul, London, 1962.

Lucas, R.   *Herbs for Healthful Living*, Arc Books, N.Y., 1969.

Martello, L.   *Witchcraft: The Old Religion*, University Books, New Jersey, 1974.

Meyer, J.   *The Herbalist*, Meyer, Indiana, 1971.

Murray, M.   *The God of the Witches*, Oxford U. Press, New York, 1970.

Ostrander, S. &   *Psychic Discoveries Behind the Iron*

Schroeder, L.   *Curtain,* Prentice Hall, New York, 1970.

Randolph, V.   *Ozark Superstitions*, Dover, New York, 1964.